MARKETING

everybody's business

DAVE NEEDHAM
ROB DRANSFIELD

Heinemann Educational,
a division of Heinemann Educational Books Ltd,
Halley Court, Jordan Hill, Oxford OX2 8EJ

OXFORD LONDON EDINBURGH
MELBOURNE SYDNEY AUCKLAND
IBADAN NAIROBI GABORONE HARARE
PARIS PORTSMOUTH NH (USA) TOKYO
SINGAPORE MADRID BOLOGNA ATHENS

© Dave Needham and Rob Dransfield 1991

First published 1991

93 94 95 11 10 9 8 7 6 5 4

British Library Cataloguing in Publication Data

Needham, David
Marketing
1. Marketing
I. Title II. Dransfield Robert
658.8

ISBN 0 435 45000 X

Designed and produced by VAP Publishing Services,
Kidlington, Oxon

Printed by Thomson Litho, Scotland

Acknowledgements

The authors and publishers would like to thank
the following people and organisations for their
help in the preparation of this book.

Margaret Berriman
Alex Clark
Marilyn Elliott
Shell Education Service
Michelle Deans
East Midlands Electricity plc
Peterborough Development Corporation
British Tourist Authority
The Rugby Football League
HP Bulmer Ltd
British Airways
Severn Valley Railway
Midland Bank plc
Manor Bakeries Ltd (a company within the
   Rank Hovis MacDougall group)
Coca-Cola Schweppes Beverages Ltd
Wanes Garages
Advertising Standards Authority
British Nuclear Fuels plc
Ark
Procter & Gamble Ltd
Ford Motor Co. Ltd
Rod Harris

Contents

Preface

In writing this book we have set out to highlight the dynamic and practical nature of marketing activities. Marketing is the essential point of contact between an organisation and its many publics in a market-place where new goods and services appear every day. At the same time today's consumers are better informed, more articulate and genuinely concerned about what has gone into a good or service before it reaches them. Therefore marketing cannot be seen as a discrete activity, to be studied separately from other business functions. It is the key strand of the very fabric of business activity that runs through the life of an organisation.

The first chapter sets out to show that marketing is a strategic process of which marketing services are the *tools* and *tactics* to support this strategic function. The student needs to be clear from the outset about the distinction between strategy and tactics, terms which originate from military use. Military strategy before and during a battle would be the general policy overview of how to defeat the enemy. Strategy involves defining the major aim and objectives as well as developing means for achieving them.

Having established its general strategy an organisation can then work out their day-to-day tools and tactics to employ to meet their strategic goals. Such tactics may change at short notice to meet changing circumstances. Tactical decisions need greater flexibility.

Effective marketing will involve providing a coherent and well planned strategy as well as tactical flexibility and clarity. It is a dynamic and sensitive area that helps to contribute to the quality, suitability and availability of the goods and services we consume.

This book sets out to provide a clear view of the background against which the concept of marketing has arisen, the various activities which best characterise marketing, and some of the ways in which marketing functions in practice in the modern economic world.

CHAPTER 1

Introducing Marketing by Michael Kirton
Director of Strategic Marketing MIM Britannia

Market influences

Today, market influences affect both the private and public sectors of our mixed economy. The key features of these influences include a market-place, prices, choice, competition and information. Such features provide a direction for all marketing activities.

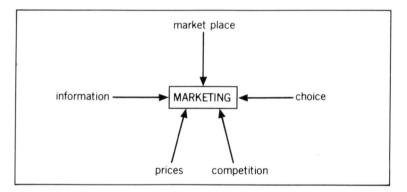

A market place describes any situation in which buyers and sellers come into contact. In most markets, buyers and sellers will meet face to face. However, in many situations today buyers and sellers do not physically 'meet'. Instead, they talk over the phone, communicate by other electronic media or correspond with each other.

Choice means that buyers and sellers have the freedom to choose with whom they deal. In particular, consumers do not have to purchase a particular model or brand. If they do not like Brand X, they can choose Brand Y or Z.

Prices act as signals in the market place. They make it possible for producers, sellers and consumers to make comparisons and form the basis for decisions. For example, if the price of one brand of soap powder increases, a consumer may decide to switch to a rival brand. If prices are high for a particular type of product, producers will be encouraged to supply more of it to the market.

Competition involves rivalry between suppliers to satisfy demand in the market place. Competition does not just involve price. It includes such things as quality, performance, service, prompt delivery and many other features which will make one product more attractive than another in the eyes of the consumer.

Information is important because it makes it possible for buyers to make 'informed' choices about their purchasing decisions. The better the information, the more opportunity there is to make informed decisions. We all know that in the modern market place there is a lot of disinformation. Advertising and promotion often disguise or distort the truth about a product. Modern products may require a lot of technical information to be conveyed to consumers. Consumers are not always in a position to decode the complex messages that are conveyed to them.

Market influences essentially rely upon the consumer to control the economy from the 'bottom up'. They are based upon the premise that for every seller there is a buyer who will determine the value of a good or service by the amount he or she is willing to pay.

The age of the consumer

Life in Western economies today is often described as taking place in a 'consumer society'. The beginning of the 'age of the consumer' is particularly associated with the period just after the Second World War. During the 1950s incomes began to increase faster than the cost of basic necessities of life and the standard of living began to rise. The shift of power from the seller to the buyer really began to bite during the 1950s as the hardships of the recent war and its immediate aftermath – for example rationing – faded into memory.

The population's desire for a higher standard of living, and therefore an increased level of consumption of consumer goods, was transformed into a reality. However, along with prosperity for the population at large, came problems for business. At long last the 'consumer was king' or, at the very least a pretty important prince – and woe betide the business that forgot it! Thus the concept of finding out what the consumer wanted, when it was wanted, from where and at what price, and the development of this information into a strategy, was born.

During this period, service industries began to serve the needs of a population with the power to buy luxury items. However, price was still an important factor because there was not a lot left over! The growth of Butlins' and Pontins' holiday camp operations are typical of this period.

Despite the fact that the population had seen a significant increase in living standards, the age of the consumer was still in its infancy. Although the consumer had surplus spending power, it was limited, and the real power still lay with the producers of cheap goods for the mass market.

The 1960s saw the shift of power begin. The 'swinging sixties' saw the consumers' muscles begin to flex with the pursuit of happiness beginning in earnest. Full employment meant high incomes, and high incomes meant high expenditure. The consumer class now included highly paid teenagers and happiness was measured in goods and leisure. To meet the demands of this new generation required a more sophisticated approach than just cutting prices.

This process has continued and gained in momentum to the present day. To find a buyer, it is no longer sufficient to have a good and simply haggle over price. In a consumer-based economy price is only one of many factors affecting the decision of the consumer.

The future

With better educated, increasingly aware and more discerning consumers, the signs are that the movement towards greater consumerism will continue to expand, not just in the West, but also to provide for the needs of the recently 'opened-up' Eastern Bloc consumers.

Task 1
Group exercise
Interview a selection of people that can clearly remember the 1950s and 1960s. In their view has power shifted away from producers and towards consumers since this time? Try to set out your research on the basis of at least ten key questions. These should try to discover such things as:

- has choice increased?
- do consumers today have more access to information?
- is there more competition in the market place?

and so on.

You should set out your findings under a heading such as 'The growth of consumer power – myth or reality?'

Task 2
Prepare a study for presentation to the group. The study should look at three different products. It should consider the way in which these products are presented. How important are factors like price, competition, choice, information and market place?

These should try to discover such things as:

- has choice increased?
- do consumers today have more access to information?
- is there more competition in the market place?

and so on.

What is marketing?

If you read the Situations Vacant columns of the newspapers, you will see many vacancies for 'marketing personnel'. Look at these extracts of advertisements taken from a recent edition of the *Sunday Telegraph* (September 1990) for the following positions:

Marketing Manager

To inspire an established sales team to produce outstanding results.

Product Manager

Responsible to the Marketing Manager, you will be responsible for the internal management of the product. You will be required to analyse market and technical trends, implementing change through development and manufacture where necessary. You will be required to present product proposals including financial aspects, together with the generation and monitoring of product plans within the overall product strategy.

Marketing Director

This is a position at the very highest level and we look to you to identify new opportunities and initiate programmes to exploit them . . . educated to degree level you must have a proven track record of effective marketing from strategy development to the preparation of a broad range of promotional and publicity materials.

So, in just three advertisements on one day, marketing was:

a selling

b the management and development of products

c the preparation of publicity material.

To discover whether marketing is, in fact **a**, **b** or **c**, or indeed a combination of these, it is helpful to examine briefly some commonly-used definitions of marketing.

Marketing – definition one

The Chartered Institute of Marketing defines marketing as:

> **'The anticipation, identification and fulfilment of a consumer need – at a profit'.**

The implication is that to pursue your corporate objectives and to continue to make a profit, you need to discover what your customers are likely to want to buy and then set out to meet their needs.

A classic example of the failure in this country to understand the importance of marketing comes from the motor cycle industry.

At the beginning of the 1950s British roads were seldom graced with the sound of a foreign motor cycle. The heavy, slow revving, large capacity machines from famous British manufacturers predominated – names like BSA, Triumph, Ariel and Norton.

Imports from Italy in the form of lightweight, high revving machines, particularly from Ducatti, were hardly given a second glance by British manufacturers – *they* didn't make them so customers couldn't have them! And, in any case, research and development costs to meet any demand for the new style machines would mean reduced profits, wouldn't they?

Someone had noticed the new machines though and thousands of miles away research and development programmes were underway. Factories were being built, workforces trained – Japan was about to enter the market!

Today, that transformation is part of recent industrial history. The motorcycles on British roads rejoice in names like Kawasaki, Honda and Suzuki and, as for the profits of British manufacturers – like most of the manufacturers themselves – they are nonexistent. By listening to the marketing missionaries, and, in effect, the consumers, the position might be very different today.

During the 1970s, marketing came to be recognised as an essential function within a successful business. However, marketing was usually a separate department in a large company, with only a tactical responsibility. To a large extent, a typical marketing department of the time busied itself with the production of advertisements and brochures, dealt with press and public relations, and generally concerned itself with the day-to-day 'image' of the company and its products.

Apart from this general, if somewhat uneasy, acceptance that marketers were necessary to handle communications, the 1970s were the decade of the accountant. The idea that 'people buy things for *their* reasons, not ours' was given little credence. At the same time rising unemployment and inflation and competitive forces from overseas causing trade imbalances, contributed to the realisation that the glorious age of a seller who held the balance of power was over. At long last the importance of marketing with its consumer-based systems began to be understood and the marketing function moved from the tactical to the strategic level in well-run businesses.

In the 1980s and 1990s marketing has come to be recognised as the discipline which co-ordinates and manages the total business function. In other words, the role of marketing has become strategic. But, if marketing is strategic, who takes care of the advertisements and public relations which many still think of as 'marketing'? The answer is **marketing services** and, at this point, we should distinguish between the two.

```
┌─────────────────────────────────────┐
│              marketing               │
│         (Strategic Function)         │
└─────────────────────────────────────┘

┌─────────────────────────────────────┐
│          marketing services          │
│          (Tools and Tactics)         │
└─────────────────────────────────────┘
```

Marketing – definition two

Marketing is an essentially strategic function concerned with ensuring that a business satisfies consumer needs profitably and at the same time outperforms rival organisations.

Marketing services

Marketing services are the tools and tactics that support marketing. Any communication with trade or consumers should ideally come under the responsibility of marketing services. The traditional areas of advertising, public relations and sales promotion are clearly marketing services. In addition, marketing services should also include the production of statements, invoices and even final demands, for the perception of the organisation, whether trade or private, is too important to be neglected.

In the 1990s, marketing is being given a far more prominent rôle in most major companies.

One can therefore ask the question, 'Is marketing . . .

a selling

b the management and development of products

c the preparation of publicity material?

It is, of course, all of these things and more. In fact, today marketing can probably best be described as the *total* business function and be defined in the following statement:

Marketing – definition three

'Marketing is the Generalship of business.'

The future

What of the future, of marketing, of business?

All that is certain is that the commercial world will become ever more competitive, the consumer ever more demanding, for the consumer's position as 'king' is becoming ever more secure as time passes by. Marketing will therefore become an ever more central activity and must involve every employee from the Managing Director downwards.

In 1985, the Chartered Institute of Marketing adopted a new slogan

'Marketing means Business' – it does.

From reading the previous section you should now be able to draw up some important definitions. Can you set out some short definitions of the following:

1 strategy

2 tactics

3 marketing

4 marketing services.

Providing for the consumer

Ultimate consumers are persons or households that buy products or consumer services for personal or family use. All consumers have needs and wants. Needs are things they must have – essentials such as food, shelter and warmth. Wants are things they can live without but which make life more comfortable or easier. Marketing draws their attention to the goods or services to satisfy such needs and wants. The ideal situation is one in which the more emphasis an organisation places upon its marketing function, the more appropriate will be the goods or service in satisfying needs and wants, and the more informed the consumer will become about any decisions they have to make.

We have seen that today many markets for goods and services have evolved to the point where the consumer has become of primary importance and has substantial control. In response to this balance of power, the successful business must produce the goods or services required to an appropriate standard at an acceptable price and distributed in a convenient manner. In terms of immediate service to the present clientele of a business, the marketing function is essential for:

> market research
> product development
> pricing
> distribution

This constitutes the tactical side of marketing and it is worth examining it in more detail at this stage.

Market research

The subject of market research could fill many volumes in its own right – it is far more complicated than asking a hundred people if they like a product and saying 'good' if sixty do. That however, is really where it all starts.

Consider bringing to market a new product and the research required to achieve success:

Stage of development	Research requirement
Product concept	Size and nature of total market. Projected profitability. Competition. Demographic trends. Production capability.
Product development	Product variations. Pricing. Packaging etc.
Advertising research	Advertisements themselves – do they work in the target market? Media selection. Other promotional techniques, direct mail, sales, promotion.
Distribution research	Distribution methods – direct, via third party, via distributors.
After-sales	Maintain contact with consumer sector to detect changes in consumer profile.

Product Development – Marketing ensures that products are developed to meet demand profitably – the aim of every business.

Pricing

Pricing is a complex area. The price weapon has many uses in business. For example:

Price structure	Possible deployment
Low prices	Seize market share. Starve competitors into vulnerability. Maintain production at full capacity.
High prices	Establish 'premium' status for product. Reduce sales to match production capacity.

Distribution

The means of effective distribution are, of course, vital to any business, but all too often they are an afterthought. For example, is a direct sales force more cost effective than using a network of agents or wholesalers? Are salespeople or distributors necessary at all or can the product or service be distributed direct to the consumer?

These questions and more need to be answered but the final solution must be cost effective to the company and acceptable to the consumer.

Marketing at the tactical level therefore ensures that a business achieves its immediate aim of satisfying its customers and making a profit – but it does *not* end there.

Strategic marketing

Marketing is now accepted in most well-run businesses as a strategic discipline or general management function and in this respect must care for the health of a business in the future – especially against competitive influences. This is because it is increasingly realised that although making a profit is important, an organisation should also develop their market share and search for brand leadership as well. So the marketer must monitor the profitability of the business and attempt to anticipate the likely trends. At the same time rival companies should be monitored and examined for vulnerable points.

Successful marketers must therefore be concerned with every aspect of their business, including future projects and other areas of their industry. Successful companies plan five, ten years and more in advance and often know more about the competition than they know about themselves!

Task
Imagine that you work in the marketing department of a company which produces washing powder. What information do you need to know about your rivals? Make a list of at least ten factors. State how each piece of information will help you with your own product.

Thinking marketing

Marketing is not just a series of business-related functions, but more wide-reaching than this. It is a business philosophy designed to develop an attitude of mind which should be shared by everyone in an organisation and is often enhanced by both frequent and open communication. Developing such an attitude of mind reduces the likelihood of crisis and contributes to the development of the overall future of an enterprise at both strategic and tactical levels.

At the heart of marketing lies the degree to which an organisation becomes marketing-orientated. The more committed a company is to its marketing activities, the more able it will be to pursue its corporate objectives and develop and retain customers. Every business in existence relies upon its customers for its survival and those who best meet customer needs will always survive a period of change.

With the accelerating increase in consumer power, the business which does not have the consumer at heart will become a dinosaur and will soon go the way of all dinosaurs!

CHAPTER 2

Understanding the Marketing Environment

It has been said that the only constant thing in life is change. Organisations today exist in a far more complex business environment than ever before and this has increased the importance of the marketing function. Influences in the environment might be friendly or hostile and pose many and varied threats and opportunities. Marketing involves understanding this changing environment so that organisations can develop their activities to deliver appropriate goods and services much more effectively than their competitors. Such an understanding should therefore be the driving force behind the decisions they make.

Interdependence

In the modern world, no individual or group can make decisions which are not affected by a wide range of external factors. The internal structure and functioning of an enterprise and the wider market and business environment in which it exists are constantly changing. Such interdependence is a basic fact of business life. Some changes are cosmetic and almost imperceptible while others, such as the takeover of another company, higher interest rates or the creation of the single market can have a dramatic impact upon an organisation's activities.

An appreciation of the importance of interdependence is vital for understanding how a business functions and which way forward it should move. A marketeer should not only be aware of his or her own market, the actions of competitors and have the ability to develop new ideas and products, but also changing business conditions within a wider environment and be able to respond with appropriate measures.

CASE STUDY

The Procter & Gamble Company

Procter & Gamble is a massive, multi-product, multi-national company which sells more than 160 brands in nearly 140 different countries. The company is a world leader in areas such as detergents, disposable nappies and health and beauty care products. In the UK, it produces numerous household brand names such as Dreft, Tide, Bold, Daz, Ariel, Fairy Liquid, Flash, Lenor, Camay, Pampers, Oil of Ulay, Head & Shoulders, Vicks and many more. At P&G they say that the winning formula for many of their market leaders has been 'the innovative adaptation of marketing experience and technology.'

At the forefront of P&G policy is the belief that ultimately 'the consumer runs the business.' This emphasises just how committed the company is to providing consumers with what they want, at a price they recognize as good value. But, in order to be able to do this, P&G, like any other company, has to consider the wider environment.

External factors

Political factors such as government policies on imports, taxes on consumption, regional grants and political stability will have an influence upon the P&G investment programme as well as economic influences such as inflation, interest rates, levels of unemployment and costs of energy. Recent international events such as those in Eastern Europe will generate an appraisal of policies alongside constantly changing local conditions such as demographic changes, skills shortages and social factors. For example, P&G has stated that they are laying the groundwork to compete more effectively in the European Community as it moves towards 1992. Examples of its activities in this direction are to be found through this book.

Consumer research

At P&G the belief is that consumer research keeps the company in touch with consumer trends and that technology creates opportunities to generate growth, and improve sales and profits. The firm also prides itself on its record for responding to consumer concerns for the environment. For example, Lenor is P&G's European fabric softener. Although consumers appreciated its performance, many did not want to buy large plastic containers. P&G responded by producing concentrated Lenor in a pouch that consumers could use to refill their containers and so met environmental concerns by significantly reducing plastic waste. Such attention to detail was recently commended by The Arthritis Foundation in America when Procter & Gamble developed a user-friendly snap-top lid for Tide powder detergent. The package is easy for anyone to use, but is especially helpful for people with arthritic hands and fingers.

Figure 2.1
Lenor in a pouch *(Source: Proctor & Gamble Ltd)*

In today's highly competitive markets P&G is aware of 'stronger global competitors developing more new products and expanding into new geographic markets throughout the world.' The company realises that the competitive challenge has never been greater and has made many organisational changes to position the company to compete more effectively in the market-place of the 1990s 'through a more focussed approach to customers and consumers alike.'

Task 1
Make a brief list of the interdependent forces highlighted in the P&G study. State briefly why each of these forces is important.

Task 2
Interview someone who works for a local organisation. Find out what outside factors affect the performance of that organisation and briefly assess how it responds to such factors.

Task 3
Comment upon whether each of the factors identified in Tasks 1 and 2 is either friendly or hostile and briefly describe the varied threats and opportunities each poses.

Task 4
Identify the advantages that P&G would seem to have over its competitors and show how it is adapting to meet new competitive challenges. What does this tell you about the company?

The P&G case study provides us with an example of how an organisation operates in a complex environment which is typically subject to constant changes outside its control. It serves to emphasize how an organisation will rely upon feedback from market research in order to be able to respond to changes in its external environment.

The market

A market is a 'collection of individuals or organisations who are actual or potential buyers of a product or service'.

Organisations tend to be classified according to the goods they produce and the markets for these goods are known as either consumer markets or industrial markets.

Consumer markets are made up of individuals who purchase items for personal or domestic consumption. Consumers typically buy from retailers and their transactions tend to be of low value. They include:

– rapid turnover consumer goods with a short shelf life, manufactured for immediate consumption, for example food and confectionery.

– durable consumer goods with a much longer life which are bought less frequently such as cars, televisions and videos.

Industrial markets consist of buyers who purchase goods and services to use towards the production of other goods or services. They include:

- industrial consumption goods which have a frequent purchase pattern but a limited life such as chemicals and lubricants.

- industrial durable goods which have a longer life such as machinery and equipment.

Some organisations sell products in both consumer and industrial markets. A motor manufacturer may produce cars for individuals to buy as well as commercial vehicles for manufacturers to use.

Though it has been the tendency in the past to title all marketing other than consumer marketing under the guise of industrial marketing, it is accepted today that these are 'organisational markets' which not only include industrial markets but also the services sector, agricultural markets and markets for the government which is an important customer for British business organisations.

Markets involve customers so an important characteristic of any market is its nature and size. For consumer goods markets, published figures on market size are normally readily obtainable. As well as this, it is possible to obtain information and statistics on areas such as:

- population size/distribution/growth

- age distribution

- changing family patterns

- social trends/fashions/aesthetic values

- trends in income and expenditure.

It is often the case that figures for organisational markets are more difficult to obtain. If a company knows the size of its market and knows that it can achieve a certain share, it can make much more accurate decisions about stock levels, production and sales forecasts. If only limited information was available it would have to invest more in primary research techniques.

CASE STUDY   National facts of tourism

The British Tourist Authority and the English Tourist Board are statutory bodies which encourage overseas visitors to Britain and British tourism within England. Research is the foundation of their marketing strategy and they carry out an extensive programme of studies. Such information is of vital use for the British tourist industry.

Look carefully at the figures extracted from some of their research.

OVERSEAS TOURISTS IN ENGLAND AND IN THE UNITED KINGDOM

millions	Trips	Nights	Spending
ENGLAND 1982	10.7	120	£2,850
1983	11.4	128	£3,625
1984	12.6	137	£4,175
1985	13.3	147	£4,925
1986	12.6	140	£4,975
1987	14.3	159	£5,675
1988	**14.5**	**154**	**£5,550**
UK TOTAL 1988	15.8	173	£6,075

OVERSEAS TOURISTS' SPENDING AND VISITS TO THE UK

In 1988 the UK earned a provisional figure of £6,075 million in foreign currency from tourism, plus £1,450 million spent by overseas visitors on travel to the UK using our passenger services. The main countries of origin of overseas visitors are shown below. There were 8.1 million trips from the European Community, earning £1,925 million.

1988 Country of origin	Trips thousands	Spending millions
USA	2,620	£1,320
France	1,970	£ 350
Federal Republic of Germany	1,830	£ 400
Irish Republic	1,250	£ 210
Netherlands	880	£ 160
Italy	660	£ 240
Canada	650	£ 250
Belgium/Luxembourg	590	£ 110
Spain	500	£ 220
Australia	480	£ 280
Middle East	470	£ 500
Switzerland	420	£ 190

ACCOMMODATION OF BRITISH TOURISTS IN ENGLAND

1988	Trips	Nights	Spending
millions	110 100%	410 100%	£6,275 100%
Accommodation used:	%	%	%
Licensed hotel	17	14	36
Unlicensed hotel or guesthouse	5	5	8
Holiday camp	3	5	5
Camping	3	4	3
Towed caravan	2	3	3
Fixed caravan	7	9	7
Rented flat or flatlet	2	2	3
Rented chalet	1	3	3
Other rented	3	5	5
Paying guest	2	2	2
With friend or relative	51	45	24
Second home	1	2	1
Boat	1	1	2
Other or in transit	2	1	1

ENGLISH HOTEL OCCUPANCY

Room Occupancy %

1978	'79	'80	'81	'82	'83	'84	'85	'86	'87	'88
54	52	50	46	47	54	57	58	57	59	60

In 1988, the average duration of stay was 2.3 nights, 18% of arrivals at English hotels were from overseas.

BRITISH TOURISTS WORLDWIDE

British residents are estimated to have spent £16,375 million in 1988 on tourism to all destinations, at home and abroad. The importance of tourism spending is illustrated below:

UK consumer's expenditure, 1988	millions
Clothes and shoes	£19,800
Energy products	£19,470
Vehicles	£18,125
TOURISM (excluding residents of Northern Ireland)	**£16,375**
Beer	£ 9,955
Home furnishings	£ 5,435

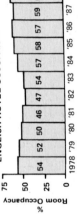

IN ENGLAND £6,275 — WALES AND SCOTLAND £1,575 — ABROAD £8,525

Figure 2.2

National facts of tourism (Source: British Tourist Authority/English Tourist Board)

BRITISH TOURISM IN ENGLAND AND BRITAIN

The following table shows the volume and value of tourism in England by British adults and the children accompanying them. A tourist trip is a stay of one night or more away from home.

millions	Trips	Nights	Spending
ENGLAND 1985	105	400	£5,075
1986	106	405	£5,600
1987	110	400	£5,550
1988	110	410	£6,275
BRITAIN 1985	126	500	£6,325
1986	128	510	£7,150
1987	132	495	£6,775
1988	130	505	£7,850

WHEN, WHERE AND HOW OF TOURISM IN ENGLAND BY BRITISH RESIDENTS

1988	All purposes	Long and short holidays	Business or conferences	Visiting friends or relatives
millions of trips	110 100%	61 100%	17 100%	29 100%
Month trip started	%	%	%	%
January-March	20	13	28	28
April-June	25	26	27	21
July	10	13	6	7
August	11	17	3	6
September	9	11	7	6
October-December	25	20	28	33
Location				
Seaside	24	36	8	9
Countryside	19	20	13	21
Small town	24	19	26	32
Large town, city	18	13	32	20
London	11	7	18	14
Other	6	7	5	4
Main transport				
Car	74	78	64	73
Bus or coach	7	9	2	10
Train	12	10	16	12
Other	6	3	18	5

Task 1

Comment generally about the changing nature of tourism within Britain during the 1980s.

Task 2

Explain briefly how the knowledge of such changes would help organisations working in the British tourist industry.

A market's size must be large enough and have sufficient purchasing power to generate profits for the organisations operating within it. Organisations prefer high growth markets because they tend to be much more profitable as opposed to fairly static or mature markets where often well-established competitors compete for limited profits by using techniques such as product differentiation, branding, advertising and price cuts.

For example, when fashion lines such as Star Wars, Transformers, My Little Pony and Masters of the Universe were introduced into the market for toys, they created vast profits for their manufacturers and stimulated the rest of the market at the same time. But as the market matured and too many similar fashion lines were introduced, profits declined and manufacturers learnt to resist the temptation to overhype 'hot' fashions.

Competition

Rarely is a product or service sold by just one business. Every organisation must be aware of its competitors. Competition is the effort of two or more businesses acting independently to sell their products to the same consumers. *Direct competition* exists when two or more organisations produce similar products and appeal to the same group of people. For example, the direct competition for Smarties is M & Ms.

Even when a business provides a unique end product with no direct competition, it still has to consider indirect competition. Consumers might examine slightly different ways of meeting the same need. Instead of buying a car, a consumer might buy a moped; instead of buying a box of chocolates they might buy a bag of sweets.

It is frequently argued that competition is good for both consumers and the business community. It forces businesses to offer new and improved products and wide selections at reasonable prices. As a result, consumers have a more varied selection of goods and services from which to choose. Without competition, consumers would have to accept a limited range of products and services at higher prices.

Understanding the behaviour of customers

The process of buying a good or service is not as simple as it might seem. People or organisations do not just go to their supplier without thinking carefully about what they want. Wherever there is choice, decisions are involved, decisions which are probably influenced by complex motives.

Markets fall into the two broad categories of consumer and organisational and the buying patterns within each are quite different.

Consumer markets

We can sum up the information gathered so far in the following few sentences.

The ultimate consumers are persons or households that purchase products or services for personal or family use. The needs and wants of consumers affect their purchasing decisions. Businesses must determine what products or services consumers need and want and then make sure these items are available. This is why organisations require detailed knowledge about the age, sex, occupation, social grouping, etc of their consumers. Such detail enables them to match the needs of each group of their consumers with an appropriate product.

Marketing therefore calls to attention such needs and enables organisations to provide goods and services in order to satisfy them. For example Iceland, the frozen food retailer, identified the need of many households for a quick method of organizing meals without the drudge of having to prepare them from scratch and identified the massive growth of the freezer market.

Much has been written about why consumers buy. There are many influences upon their behaviour and these all affect each individual in a slightly different way.

A group of important factors which clearly affect consumer behaviour are the **economic determinants of consumer demand**. These include:

- the real disposable incomes available to consumers to spend on goods and services. An increase in real incomes will generally increase the demand for goods and services unless a commodity is an inferior one. (eg synthetic fibre clothing.)

- the relative prices of substitute products whose purchase might be preferred or seen as better value for money.

- population size or composition could affect the demand for products. For example, if the birth rate increased, Mothercare products would be in greater demand.

- government influences in areas such as credit regulations and safety requirements could influence demand for a host of commodities.

- tastes, fashions and habits, which constantly influence the pattern of demand for goods and services. Pepsi Cola appealed to tastes with a first in the advertising world by presenting a preview of Madonna's new album *Like a Prayer* in a two-minute Pepsi commercial.

Another area that the marketer must understand are the needs or wants that inspire **individual motivation** and give rise to particular forms of purchase behaviour. The best known theory of motivation is that of Abraham Maslow who

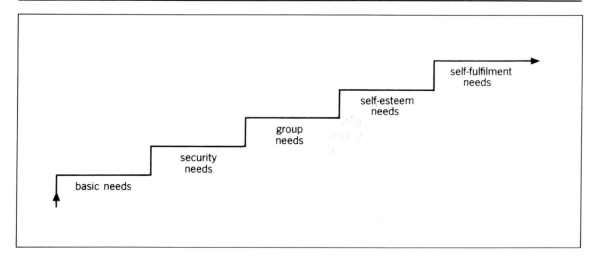

Figure 2.3
Abraham Maslow's hierarchy of needs

suggested that although it is difficult to analyse individual needs, it is possible to develop a hierarchical picture which can be split into five broad categories.

- Security needs are concerned with physical well-being and the need to provide protection, perhaps with a house in a safe trouble-free environment, with protected and reliable items within it.

- Group needs would centre on the desire for acceptance, the need for affiliation and purchases associated with belonging to a community.

- Self-esteem needs would stem from one's desire for status, for a sense of achievement and for respect for one's accomplishments. This might lead to the possession of prestigious items, through living a lavish lifestyle, or self-esteem generated, for example, through making donations to charities.

- Self-fulfilment is concerned with full personal development and individual creativity. To achieve this level individuals would be trying to ensure that their individual skills and capacities were being totally utilised.

The implications of this theory are easy to perceive as different products and services are related to different needs, eg., life insurance is rooted in a desire for safety, a BMW related to self-esteem needs etc. It is noticeable that in Western societies there are far more products related to self-fulfilment needs than in third world countries. Such a theory helps an organisation to bear the consumer more closely in mind when undertaking marketing and advertising activity.

Another theory of motivation is the **self image theory**. The 'self' is an individual's image of himself or herself. Within this 'self' there are various ways to maintain and enhance this image. The individual will make choices of car, music, clothing, places to shop which will fit into his or her perception of 'self.' By discovering how customers wish themselves to be perceived in terms of an image, organisations can design, promote and retail goods which are consistent with those sought by prospective purchasers.

CASE STUDY

Shaping an image

TSB, the UK's fifth largest bank has recently mounted a massive bid to shed its down-market image and propel itself into the 'top league'. The priority has been to emphasize the financial services on offer and move away from the dowdy traditional association with savings.

Adidas, the market leader in sports goods, has shifted its fashion development centre to Paris and hopes to give its textiles a top fashion image by engaging French design talent.

Fabergé has moved into the market for shampoo targeted specifically at teenagers. The target market will be 12 to 19 year olds. The four brands – Ritzy, Hot Tropics, Rugged Herbal and Cool Mint will be aimed at different lifestyles.

The **Rugby League** has recently invested in two officially registered logos to give the traditional working class sport a 'glossier image', particularly in the South, as well as to earn profit which can be ploughed back into the game.

Figure 2.4
The two new Rugby League logos
(Source: The Rugby Football League)

Task 1
Describe briefly what each of the organisations in the case study is trying to do and explain what sort of interested parties/prospective purchasers they are likely to attract.

Task 2
Think carefully about the products and services you regularly purchase. Choose two that you feel identify with your own self-image and explain why you feel that they do so.

Building up a consumer profile

One important area of interest to the marketeer is the need to understand the *personality* of their customers. If any of their customers have similar personalities, then it may be possible to divide the market up on the basis of such stereotypes. For example, various models of cars, records and fashion products all reflect the personality traits of customers. Boots No 17 teenage cosmetic brands has traditionally been targeted at 18 to 24 years olds and has had a fun, fashionable and experimental image. As demographic changes in the 1990s will see fewer teenagers, Boots is changing its products to appeal to the more mature personality. The new version will appeal to the older, budget-conscious conservative consumer.

Culture encompasses standard patterns of behaviour and also plays an important rôle in shaping our purchase patterns. It stems from the traditions, beliefs and values of the community in which we live. For example, the consumption of alcohol is an essential feature of western life. It is however forbidden to Muslim communities. Though a nation might be characterised by one culture, there may be a series of sub-cultures existing within it. Sub-cultures are important for organisations who wish to target their brands to those who share the values of that particular sub-culture. For example, youth markets, ethnic groups, senior citizens, etc.

Socio-economic grouping

Expenditure and consumption patterns can be broken up according to the *social class* of the consumer. Dividing groups up into different classes is called **social stratification**. Each class will have its own pattern of behaviour which will serve to reinforce its purchasing and consumption patterns. Socio-economic groups classify people according to their similarity of income, occupation and education. One of the best known classifications used to divide the UK is as follows:

Socio-economic group	Social class	Type of occupation	Example
A	Upper/upper-middle class	higher managerial, administrative, professional	surgeon, director of a large company
B	Middle class	intermediate managerial, professional, administrative	bank manager, headteacher, surveyor
C1	Lower middle class	supervisory, junior managerial or administrative, clerical	bank clerk, nurse, teacher, estate agent
C2	Skilled working class	skilled manual workers	joiner, welder, foreman
D	Working class	semi-skilled and unskilled	driver, postman, porter
E	Those at lowest level of subsistence	low paid/unemployed	casual workers, state pensioners, unemployed

Figure 2.5
Socio-economic classifications

Socio-economic grouping provides a reliable picture of the relationship between occupation and income. Members of each group will have similar priorities in behaviour which will influence their needs. For example we would expect A, B, C1s to spend some of their income on private education, private health care, new cars, antiques etc, whereas C2, D's and E's would spend a significantly higher proportion of their income on necessities.

Over recent years, organisations have paid increasing attention to the *life-style* of their consumers. A life-style is a behaviour pattern adopted by a particular community or a sub-section of it. By understanding such a life-style, they can develop products and target them to this group. For example someone upwardly mobile and ambitious would seek an affluent life-style and a higher material standard of living. The UK 'Yuppy' is reputed to be a young (24–35), well educated and upwardly mobile professional. Affluence comes from working hard in particular areas, eg high finance, and is spent on expensive clothes, cars and homes in high-status districts. In contrast, traditionalists would wish to conform to group norms for social approval.

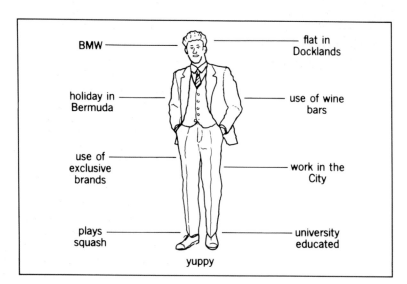

Figure 2.6
The image created by the term 'Yuppy'

Some advertising agencies construct life-style categories to advise their clients on how to design and position new products to appeal to groups with similar life-style patterns.

CASE STUDY   Analysing an advertisement

Select an advertisement from a newspaper as well as one from a magazine that you regularly read.

Task 1
Comment briefly upon the nature of the product or service featured in the advertisement.

Task 2

Explain how the advertiser tries to appeal to potential customers. Refer to:

a consumer motivations

b the consumer's personality

c the culture of the consumer

d their social class

e their life-style.

Task 3

Outline whether you feel that the advertiser shows a sound understanding of the behaviour of the consumer. Report your findings back to your teaching group.

Organisational markets

Every day in towns and cities across the United Kingdom, car dealers hand the keys of new cars to their customers. A complex manufactured product such as this will be made up of numerous parts and materials from numerous suppliers. Whereas it is easy to imagine the sale of a car from a showroom, we tend not to think of the vast number of sales transactions which have taken place beforehand to bring together the components to manufacture the car.

An organisational market is a market where organisations buy products and services which are used directly or indirectly in the production of other goods and services or are to be resold.

Most people are unaware of the significance of the organisational market. Consider again the number of transactions required to manufacture a car. Iron ore is mined and transported to a plant to be made into steel. The steel is bought and formed into the chassis and body. In order to construct a car with about 12 000 different parts, a manufacturer will probably produce about 6000 and buy the other 6000 from other companies. Many of these companies will only supply one part, so they will have to buy components from several thousand companies. The companies supplying these parts will also have suppliers from whom they buy raw materials and components. Ford is the biggest purchaser in the British motor industry with purchases close to one and a half billion pounds per annum as well as several hundred million pounds worth of purchases from Ford companies abroad. Ford is also the biggest single customer of the British machine tool manufacturing industry, its orders exceeding the rest of the motor industry put together.

When a company is selling to other organisations it still needs to understand the behaviour of its customers, but whereas a consumer product might have a potential market of 56 million users, the total number of organisations in the UK is less than 3 million and the likelihood is that the product on offer will only appeal to a very small number of organisations.

The demand for organisational products and services is called **derived demand** because the amount purchased is determined by the demand for related goods and services. For example, the number of tyres purchased by a motor manufacturer will depend upon the demand for vehicles. The industrial supplier is therefore aware that they are supplying goods or services to help produce someone else's product so that the demands of the final customer can be met.

Depending upon derived demand can have serious limitations. Organisational markets are subject to **business cycles** and the demand for industrial products and services may fluctuate violently when the pace of business activity changes. Recessionary economic conditions can therefore lead to severe cut-backs in derived demand for inputs and cause a business to close down plants and lay off workers.

Companies supplying goods in organisational markets face constantly changing circumstances which are often called **contingency factors**. Marketing departments need to be constantly aware of information relating to such specific conditions. For example:

- the average value of an order follows a lengthy negotiation period and credit facilities will be very important.

- there is a risk of a takeover by the customer.

- buyers often deliberately exercise buying power to influence the conditions of supply such as terms and prices.

- large companies often seek small companies to exercise their buying power.

- large buyers may pursue a deliberate policy of delaying payment for goods and services received. This can have serious implications for the cashflow of suppliers.

- risk of supplier dependency on customer.

Vertical and horizontal markets

Organisational markets are described as either vertical or horizontal. Where an organisational product or service is used by only a small number of buyers, it has a **vertical market**. For example there are very few buyers of passenger aircraft or electric locomotives. An organisational product has a **horizontal market** if it is purchased by many different kinds of organisations in many different industries. For instance the supply of stationery and lubricants has a broad usage.

The process of selling in an organisational market differs widely from selling in consumer markets. Selling can often require expert technical knowledge, particularly if products

Figure 2.7
Vertical market

Figure 2.8
Horizontal market

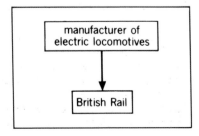

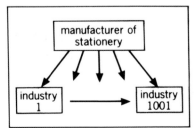

are complex or specifications need to be altered. Decisions may also involve numerous people across a range of departments. For example, the purchase of a computer may involve discussions by representatives from a range of departments likely to be using the machine. Whereas consumers are influenced by a variety of behaviour factors, the main concern of most organisational customers is to obtain the necessary products at the lowest possible costs.

CASE STUDY

Marks & Spencer

M&S owns no factories nor does it make any of the goods that it sells. The firm works with manufacturers who supply to the company's high specifications. M&S set up this practice of direct dealing with producers in the 1920s. It is openly proud of the 'personal and friendly' relations it has with suppliers as not only does this help speed the response to customer needs, it also helps to anticipate them.

Sales of clothing account for almost half of the £5 billion plus turnover at M&S. To maintain such a position, numerous suppliers create new lines and ranges. Highly experienced buying teams determine the specifications for new lines, assess the suppliers' ability to produce the manufactured goods, and negotiate price, quantity and delivery. Many of the suppliers have worked with M&S for a considerable number of years and have seen their businesses grow in a similar fashion — although maybe not to similar proportions!

Task 1
List the benefits available to a small garments manufacturer of supplying goods to M&S.

Task 2
What factors must such a small business take into consideration and be aware of when supplying to such a large organisation? Are there any dangers involved?

Task 3
If you were working for a marketing department, would you prefer to be involved in marketing consumer products or services or industrial products and services? Support your answer with an explanation.

Task 4
Comment generally on the sort of image generated by M&S. What type of customer are their clothing products directed at?

Market segmentation

Different customers exhibit different needs, wants, desires, dislikes and likes. Not every person likes the same make of motor car or has the same taste in clothes. If cost and production time were of no importance, manufacturers would make products to the exact specifications of each buyer. Unfortunately, this is not at all practical. A business cannot provide a different product for each customer. On the other hand, neither can it serve its customers successfully if it groups all of their needs and wants together. To solve this dilemma an organisation uses market segmentation.

Instead of trying to serve all consumers, an organisation will focus its efforts on a single part of the total market. Within a total market it is possible to group customers with similar characteristics into **market segments**. Market segmentation is therefore a process of identifying and then dividing and separating a total market into parts so that different strategies can be used for different sets of customers.

Task 4 of the previous case study asked you what sort of image M&S portrays and the type of customer its clothing products are directed at. The M&S image is one of a concern caring for customers, staff, quality and also the community in which they trade. The bulk of their clothing products are directed at an upper market segment primarily for those between the ages of 35 and 55.

Market segmentation is an important feature for setting marketing objectives. It enables an organisation to position ranges of brands and product varieties. For example, markets consist of competing brands. A marketing department will try to establish a particular position in the market for their brand, eg upmarket, midmarket, downmarket. In the market for furniture polish the upmarket brand is Pledge; in the midmarket is Mr Sheen and in the downmarket position is Sparkle. Segmentation also enables organisations to identify particular gaps which offer prime opportunities for expansion.

CASE STUDY   The Selfridge Selection

In the past, exclusivity and mail order have sounded a bit like a contradiction but Selfridges combined the two with the launch of the up-market Selfridge Selection.

The Selfridge Selection aimed to overcome the social stigma of mail order. Most mail order in the UK is generated by seven catalogue companies whose core market lies firmly in the lower socio-demographic sectors of the population. 'Next' has been the exception to this and probably contributed most to the shift in status for home shopping. 'Next' made shopping through the post fashionable among the young and trendy who were wooed by the stylish advertisements and the coffee table fashion magazine.

At Selfridges it is felt that the opportunity to sell expensive items through the post has always existed but that, apart from 'Next', no-one has pursued it intelligently because the perception of mail order is downmarket and retailers would be worried about a negative reaction.

The Selfridge Selection will only offer the most exclusive and best-selling lines. They will be despatched in boxes, packed in white tissue (which will be ideal for gifts), within 48 hours, to any address, with a lifetime guarantee promising a cash refund with 'no questions asked.'

Though the future for this new concept of mail order in the UK looks strong, development will not be an easy ride and the European giants and US companies which are already established in this field will look on with interest.

Task 1
What would you expect to be the characteristics or needs of buyers in the market segment that Selfridges are gearing their efforts towards?

Task 2
Explain how these characteristics and needs differ from those within other segments of the mail order market.

Distinguishing between the different characteristics and needs of consumers in order to identify a particular market segment is known as the process of **differentiation**. In order to identify differences amongst potential buyers it is often practical to ask a series of what, how, where, when, why and who questions.

For example

- *What* needs do buyers wish to satisfy with the purchase of a product? What influences their demand and causes them to buy more or less?
- *How* would consumers or organisations buy the product or service? How do they use the product? How much have they to spend?
- *Where* do they purchase the product? Where do customers obtain information?
- *When* do customers decide to buy? When do customers buy more or less of the service?
- *Why* are customers motivated to buy? Why do they prefer a particular organisation's services?
- *Who* are the customers? Who are the competition?

In order for any segment which is identified to be useful, it must be large enough and have sufficient **purchasing power** within it to generate a desirable profit for the producer. It must also be *accessible* through the channels of distribution and be *responsive* to the marketing of a new product or service.

Almost any factor that distinguishes between customers can be used to segment a market.

Geographic segmentation

This involves the division of markets into groups by location. Though this has more obvious implications for overseas markets, even within a country substantial regional differences concerning climate and social custom will affect customer purchases. For example, there are vast differences in UK consumption habits in areas such as bakery products, heating systems and alcohol consumption.

Demographic segmentation

This involves dividing the consumer market into groups using population data. Age may indicate whether a person is interested in buying a product or service. Families with infants will purchase baby foods, cots and baby clothes. Children may influence their parents' decisions about toys and equipment. Teenagers tend to buy records and clothing. Young adults will buy products and services relating to leisure and setting up their own household. Young middle-aged adults spend time and money replacing items they bought in their twenties, as fashions change. Older middle-aged adults are often financially secure and at the peak of their earning potential. Manufacturers of various products and services are today spending more time developing goods for the expanding senior citizen sector in the UK.

Another obvious way of segmenting a market is by gender. Many products are for men or women only. Population data also reveals income levels. What and how much people spend is related to their income. Social stratification (see page 19) takes into account both income and levels of education to provide a clearer picture of the divisions in a market.

Psychographic segmentation

Another method of classifying customers into a potential market is by using psychographic segmentation. Though this sounds rather imposing, it simply involves looking at a combination of demographic and behavioural patterns to understand more about the personality of the buyer. For example, purchasing on the basis of thrift, to experiment with a product, to purchase a bargain or to exhibit loyalty to a product. Lifestyle segmentation is an extension of this idea and is based upon the particular way of life and values that certain groups of people have. It might include areas such as fashion, interests, health, hygiene, religion, social issues and morals. All of these issues are of importance to certain groups of people and help to pick out groups or segments to target goods and services at.

Some markets are segmented in terms of *benefits* being sought by customers. Some might buy a product for its looks, others for its flavour, its ease of use, effectiveness etc.

Segmentation in organisational markets

Just like the consumer market, the broad market for organisational products and services is of little value unless it is broken up into segments. Organisations in horizontal markets will find segmentation easier to apply than those in vertical markets for whom the outlets are more limited. Factors such as the type of use, the rate at which a product or service is required, geographic location and the Standard Industrial Classification (SIC) will all influence segmentation.

Having targeted one or more segments organisations should develop a strategy to reflect their product attributes or differences which are appropriate to each targeted segment. Even within a logically defined segment in the market all buyers might not be the same and an organisation will have to decide how to position the product within this segment to influence its consumer profile in relation to its rival products.

CASE STUDY   ## The Cola War

The battle between two distinguished giants, Coca-Cola/Pepsi-Cola, is a predictable marketing story based upon a hard-fought clash for market share which has been built upon an attempt to differentiate between relatively similar brands through heavy image-orientated advertising.

Whereas four in ten US beverages are carbonated soft drinks, the figure is only 8% in the UK. One claim is that Coke is bigger than tap water in the US!

Both Coca-Cola and Pepsi-Cola have busily segmented their market. Coke has DietCola, CherryCola, Caffeine Free Diet Cola, orange Fanta, lemon and lime Sprite and Lilt. Pepsi has CherryPepsi, DietPepsi, 7-Up, Diet 7-Up and Tango.

The conflict which obsesses both organisations is the need to appear exciting, different and even glamorous. Both brands have captured the imaginations of millions, for example, Pepsi, with advertisements featuring superstar Michael Jackson and Coke with its themes of American nationhood.

The key to the new Pepsi strategy is advertisements that depict young people choosing Pepsi above other colas as well as continuing pop star involvement, while Coke opt for attractive young people enjoying life whilst drinking Coke, to bring out a blend of music, sport and fashion.

Figure 2.9
Coke opt for attractive young people enjoying life *(Source: Coca-Cola Schweppes Beverages Ltd)*

Task 1
Comment upon how both Coke and Pepsi have segmented their market. What type of consumer is each market segment geared towards?

Task 2
Why do you feel that carbonated soft drinks do not sell as well in this country as they do in the US?

Task 3
In your opinion, how successful have both brands been in capturing the imagination of consumers?

Do you think that their advertisements could have been more appropriately targeted and their products more successfully positioned?

Comment upon your findings. Have you any suggestions for how each could improve their strategy?

CHAPTER 3

Researching the Market

The American Marketing Association uses a simple working definition of market research:

> The systematic gathering, recording and analysing of data about problems relating to the marketing of goods and services.

We can break down this definition into its important ingredients:

Systematic	– in other words, using an organised and clear method or system.
Gathering	– knowing what you are looking for, and collecting appropriate information.
Recording	– keeping clear, and organised records of what you find out.
Analysing	– ordering and making sense of your information in order to draw out relevant trends and conclusions.
Problems relating to marketing	– finding out the answers to questions which will help you to understand better your customers and other details about the market place.

It is the business of the marketing research function within a large organisation to know as much as they possibly can about customers, markets and products.

In order to sell to people

● what they want to buy

● when they want to buy it

it is essential to build up a profile of these customers, what they do, when and why they do it, and what would encourage them to use your products and services.

Market research also needs to find out what might make customers choose a rival product in preference to your own. For example, is it as a result of changes in demand, the existence of an aggressive competitor, or poor service on your part?

One of the best ways to understand the market in which you operate and your current level of success in that market is to make a detailed examination of your own customers, their relationship with your business, as well as to study their habits and motivations.

Who better to know a company's relationship with its customers than itself?

Internal and external information

Internal information

Much of the information that an organisation requires about the market place is held internally by various different departments within the organisation.

The relationship with a customer starts with a name, address, and the nature of the property – whether it is a home or a business. Once the market research function has received these details it gives to these people a unique reference number at the relevant address called a **CUSTOMER REFERENCE NUMBER**, (CRN).

The CRN is crucial to all dealings with that customer, and it is with reference to the CRN that many of the financial transactions take place.

We can see the importance of the CRN in terms of the collection of appropriate marketing information by reference to a large company selling electricity to domestic and industrial users. To the CRN the company can attach all manner of information held internally that tells it more about that particular customer, for example:

Tariff Type – the price a customer pays for electricity can vary according to whether they are a home or business, a large or small customer. Profitability to the electricity company will vary accordingly to the type of customer.

Consumption – the company can track the amount of electricity a customer uses and when they use it.

Method of payment – some people prefer prepayment rather than credit, others prefer to pay monthly rather than quarterly.

Change of tenancy – the company knows when people move out of and into a property when they ask for a final reading for the supply of electricity.

New buildings – the company knows when and where new buildings that use electricity are being erected because they apply for electricity supply.

Internal information has a valuable second purpose, and that is to know as much as possible about the company's capability for fulfilling the demands within the market and potential outside that market.

So, armed with all this internal information, the company can portray an accurate picture of its customers and how they interrelate.

However, this isn't enough for a company that wants to develop new markets and design new products for its existing customers.

What else does it need to know?

External information

The internal information that has been collated needs to be put into context, as on its own it simply provides a snapshot of the organisation and its customers. It tells the organisation nothing about how effective its performance is, relative to competitor organisations, nor how business could be threatened by those competitors.

External sources of information give another dimension to the data that makes it far more valuable when making marketing decisions. It is used in two main ways.

First, outside information simply enhances the existing knowledge of a company's customers. For example, postcodes will help them to group customers geographically, and also, by identifying and labelling certain characteristics about their customers a company can make assumptions concerning their customer's needs. Two examples of useful external sources are

- Domestic socio-economic data – customers are classified by their house type, the assumption being that a certain lifestyle is associated with that type of house.

- Industrial classification – business customers can be classified according to the type of business they are, the assumption here being that certain businesses can be broadly defined as using particular products or processes and having predictable demands for products and services.

Secondly, external sources can complement a company's own information, by providing direct comparison with competitors, by putting its performance within the context of the economy as a whole, and by identifying gaps offering potential.

For example, an increase in the sales of a particular branded chocolate is not good news for the company involved if the increase in a competitors' sales are greater. The additional information about competitors' performance tells a company whether it is gaining or losing market share.

Internal data	
purchasing	stock levels, unit costs, usage rates
production	output, material, labour inventory, physical distribution, overheads, machine use
personnel	wage costs, efficiency levels, absenteeism, staff turnover
marketing	promotional and administration expenditures, brand and market data
sales	measured by product volumes, value, contribution, order size
finance	cost and accounting data

External data
Government sources (a brief guide to government sources is given in 'Government Statistics' available from Government Statistical service.)
Research organisations, eg universities and polytechnics.
Trade Associations, eg NHBC, ABTA, etc.
Journals and specialist publications.
Commercial Research Organisations, eg MINTEL, Gallup, Nielsen.
Directories. A detailed list of major statistical works and other publications is provided by HMSO, called Official Statistics. Foreign Sources are listed in the Stationery Office publication "International Organisations and Overseas Agencies and Publications".

Figure 3.1
Important sources of internal and external data

Task 1
A large High Street retailer of menswear wants to research the public's perception of its range. It hires a Market Research Agency to do the work. What sources of information will the Agency use which are

a internal to the retail company

b external to the retail company?

Primary and secondary data

Despite coming from many difference places, all data can be categorised as either primary or secondary information. Each has its benefits and drawbacks, but together they can provide a fuller picture of the market.

Primary data

This is information that is first hand knowledge, 'straight from the horse's mouth.' Any information a company compiles from its own activities is primary data. Its own research findings would also be classified as primary information.

Secondary data

As soon as primary data is published it becomes secondary data. So, a market researcher making a comparative study of the various companies within the fuel industry will use secondary sources of data (albeit taken from primary data), unless he conducts his own market research amongst those companies.

These definitions, however are not always so clear cut. Internally, primary data will be the information each department holds concerning its own activities. This may be collated into secondary data by a Public Relations department and published externally.

The main benefit of primary information is that, coming from the source itself it is likely to be accurate. However, one drawback can be that it is only relevant to the activity for which it was initially intended, and any adaption may affect its accuracy.

The benefit of secondary information is that it can frequently offer different interpretations of the same information. Therefore information concerning the company's performance can mean one thing to a financial analyst concerned with profitability and another to a business analyst concerned with operating efficiency. However, the obvious drawback with secondary information is that it can be open to misinterpretation through subjective analysis.

Qualitative and quantitative data

The most important thing to remember is that what comes out of market research is only as good as what goes in, therefore the structure of the questions, the sample size and type, and the nature of the questioning should all be carefully considered before any project proceeds.

The difference between qualitative and quantitative data can be broadly summarised as follows:

- qualitative information gives opinions
- quantitative information gives facts.

Qualitative information often provides the context within which the quantitative facts operate.

Best done on a face-to-face basis, qualitative information is frequently established through general discussion.

The, 'What do you think about. . . . ?' approach gives people the opportunity to offer a variety of different opinions, reasons, motivations and influencing factors that prompt them to hold their opinions. A group discussion allows different opinions to be offered which will frequently reach a consensus, giving an idea of the popular view. People enjoy offering their opinions on subjects as diverse as the current political climate to the taste of a particular margarine, and what it gives the researcher is an overall view of that particular audience's reaction to his proposition. As with all research, it is vital that the audience is carefully selected to provide relevant replies. For instance, if you are sounding out large cereal farmers' opinions of their advisory body with particular reference to grain-drying techniques, the sample chosen for the research should reflect that and be composed of large cereal farmers.

Frequently, however it provides a useful perspective to have a control group. Therefore a second non-target group may be added to the sample, perhaps in this case, composed of all cereal farmers.

This will often provide direction for the more precise quantitative research which will give depth to any particular aspect of the qualitative work. Quantitative research is most effective where there is little room for opinion, usually through the interview technique. This can often be conducted by telephone.

Let's return to the previous example, then, the large cereal farmers' opinion of the agricultural advisory service with regard to advice that can be given on grain-drying techniques.

The quantitative work will be conducted within the target group, the large cereal farmers. It may be used to establish with which fuel they dry their grain, when, for how long, at what temperature. They may also be asked whether they know of the advisory service, if they have ever used it, and whether they were satisfied.

What all this will tell the company is whether the way in which they market and run the service is effective in getting the message across. If the research findings say 'no', the qualitative research will help to identify why, which can then be further investigated by the quantitative aspects of the work.

CASE STUDY   How British Rail researched its InterCity Business Service

In the 1980s, British Rail carried out extensive research into its InterCity Business Service in order to improve its service and make it more competitive with major rivals. Analysis of the results of the survey revealed a need to reposition the service. A major part of the research was to try and discover which features of rail travel were seen as advantages and which features as disadvantages.

To find out why people used different forms of transport, discussion groups were held between InterCity, car and plane users. The results of this research revealed a complicated picture of why different people used different services — what to one person was seen as an advantage, to another was unacceptable.

Mode of transport	Benefits mentioned by users
Car	privacy flexibility accessibility control over journey speed
Plane	standard of service thrill of flying arrive fresh
InterCity	the space to move around the ability to work while travelling centre to centre

Figure 3.2
Results of discussions between different types of business travellers

The major finding of this research was that for the business traveller, the key factor influencing their views of the different modes of transport was the status accompanying their choice of transport.

Having identified through customer research areas of dissatisfaction with its service, InterCity has been able to set about revitalising its business travel. InterCity has designed a package aimed at improving the facilities on business travel by rail, emphasising features such as lack of strain, the space to move around and the ability to work while travelling.

Task 1
Describe how British Rail could have used

a qualitative research

b quantitative reseach

to chart transport users' views.

Task 2
Set up your own discussion group with a small selection of business travellers.

What are their views about alternative forms of business travel?

Are they similar or different to the British Rail findings?

What are their views of British Rail's revamped business service?

To set up this exercise you will need to arrange your classroom so that the discussion can take place in the centre of the room. Invite four appropriate visitors into the class. They should sit as part of a small circle with up to six student interviewers. The rest of the class should be positioned around the edge of the circle as 'listeners in' and take notes of relevant points that are made.

Social grades/socio economic groups

For market research to be effective, it is vital that the market is segmented into a manageable size (see Chapter 2). There are several market segmentation techniques, but they must all take account of the fact that those within any segment have certain definitive characteristics.

Why is market segmentation useful to a marketer?

If your service is a local one you do not want to offer it nationally; if you sell ladies' fashions, you do not want to sell to men; if you offer a business service you do not want to offer that to the domestic market; and if you offer a very exclusive, expensive product you will not find many buyers amongst the general public.

Targeting by market segmentation has been likened to firing a rifle rather than a blunderbuss. A blunderbuss fires shots everywhere, peppering the whole market, whereas a rifle with accurate sights will hit the target you are aiming at.

For example, the business market is divided by the nature of its work into commercial and industrial activities. Within those two groups, customers will be further subdivided into the types of business, shops, offices, warehouses etc. To take that one step further, they will be subdivided into the types of shop – hairdressers, pizza parlours, estate agents, etc.

The domestic market, or general public, is divided differently. The most frequently encountered is social grading, based on the type of job people do. (see Socio-economic groups Chapter 2). The underlying assumption is that particular jobs have certain lifestyles attached to them, in part defined by the disposable income available to workers within those categories. By classifying the public in this way, an exclusive product would be marketed to groups A & B because they are the most likely to be able to afford it, and consider it a worthwhile investment.

Most of the British population fall into groups C1, C2, D. However, further categories can be defined to help target your message even more accurately.

Housing types are often assumed to have different lifestyles attached to them, and the occupants have different levels of spending power. The accent on spending in a high-rise council flat is likely to be different to that in the large detached four-bedroom house. One will be more receptive to an exclusive product than the other.

The fundamental flaw with all socio-economic segmentation is the assumption that a certain job or house brings with it a certain spending power. History tells us that there have been as many poverty-stricken dukes as rags-to-riches market traders. In addition, those within a lower socio-economic group will very often have aspirations to a higher group.

The type of grouping that is used by market researchers is often dependent on the market that is being researched. For example, with the development of the Single Market a number of large companies have been moving towards

Eurobranding. Market research has focussed on distinct types of households or groups within Europe. Research can then be focussed on these distinct groups which are identified according to socio-economic characteristics as well as other features. (Other researchers argue that this approach is too simplistic because there are no typical Europeans, regional differences can be as marked as international similarities).

Sagacity life cycle groupings

Another type of grouping which has proved popular with market researchers has been that of Sagacity Life Cycle Groupings. The basic idea behind Sagacity grouping is that people have different behavioural patterns and aspirations as they go through life. Four main stages of life cycle are defined which are then further sub-divided according to income and occupation groups (see figure 3.3).

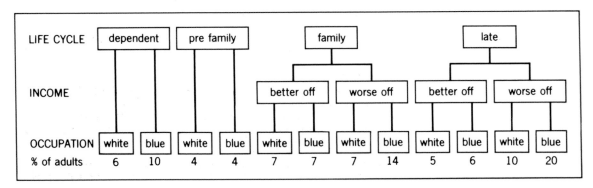

Figure 3.3
Sagacity Life Cycle Groupings

Definition of life cycle stages

Dependent – Mainly under 24s, living at home or full-time student.

Pre-family – Under 35s, who have established their own household but have no children.

Family – Parents, under 65, with one or more children in the household.

Late – Includes all adults whose children have left home or who are over 35 and childless.

Definitions of occupation groups

White – Head of household is in the ABC1 occupation group.

Blue – Head of household is in the C2DE occupation group.

Task 1

What are the advantages and disadvantages of using socio-economic groups as a means of sorting people in order to carry out market research?

Is it possible to refine such groupings?

What alternative methods can you think of?

Techniques

Different techniques will bring different results in marketing research.

Factual information is most easily and valuably collected where there is little room for opinion to be expressed, say by the questionnaire.

Opinions, feelings, attitudes are most usefully established through discussion groups, conducted within the target sample who will often bounce ideas off one another until a consensus is reached.

Four main avenues of communication are open to the market researcher:

- face-to-face
- telephone
- postal
- desk research.

Each has its benefits and its drawbacks, which can be seen by a closer examination:

Face-to-face
is the best contact available. It allows two-way communication between the researcher and researched. It is flexible in that gestures, facial expressions, signs of impatience, and boredom can all be noted. However, even face-to-face contact can vary enormously.

A questionnaire in the street is less friendly and detailed than a group discussion in the home. Each will invariably yield different results. A street interview will be brief, impersonal, using a broadly defined sample group whereas a home discussion can be exactly the opposite – detailed, personal, and a tightly-defined sample group.

Telephone
is frequently more appropriate for business interviews as the recipient is often busy, and unavailable for group discussion. However, it is often regarded as intrusive since it catches people unawares, especially in the home. This means that the respondent can start the interview with a negative view, which questioning will not necessarily help to overcome. However, it is a cost effective means of reaching people, and the replies received are likely to be truthful. The rate of response will probably be higher than the third, postal technique.

Postal
the level of response to a questionnaire sent by mail will vary enormously depending on its relevance to the reader and their interest in making their opinions known.

Response rates are often as low as 10–20%, and therefore may not constitute a particularly representative group – they might just be representative of those who like filling in forms! The way to avoid this mishap is to ensure that the questionnaire is brief, succinct and sent only to those to whom it is directly relevant. A good postal questionnaire can achieve as high as a 60–70% response rate.

Desk research

involves researching secondary sources of data. Since most of this can be searched out by telephone, post and computer link, the majority of the work is conducted from your desk.

Other research techniques are often used to establish attitudes and opinions. These are outlined briefly below:

Hall tests

hire a hall, display various, (usually consumer) products or services, even potential advertisements, inviting participants' views.

Testing

can help to establish customers' views within a limited area before a national or regional launch of a new product, service or advertisement. In the case of industrial products and processes, a test market may be as small as a single company whereas with a consumer product, it may be a whole county or more.

Panels

use the same group of people over a period of time to establish a market's changing attitudes to the same products.

Preparing a questionnaire

A questionnaire is a systematic list of questions designed to obtain information from people about:

- specific events
- their attitudes
- their values
- their beliefs.

Always make sure that the person answering the questions knows exactly the purpose of the exercise and is willing to co-operate.

Though it is easy to think up questions, it is very difficult to produce a good questionnaire.

Activity

Study the following questionnaire on kettles either on your own or as a group. The questionnaire is not very effective, for a variety of reasons. Highlight as many weaknesses as possible.

What do you think the purpose of the questionnaire is? Rewrite the questionnaire, suggesting ways of making it more effective, in terms of the questions it asks and its layout.

In preparing a questionnaire you should make your introduction simple and your layout clear. Try to anticipate any possible misunderstandings. You want the questionnaire to provide you with the information you need. Do not include

Kettle Ownership Questionnaire

Name .... Address ....
.... Telephone Number ......

1 Do you use a kettle? Yes/No

2 What make is it? ....

3 Have you had other kettles before? ....

4 Which of them was best? ....

5 Have kettles that you bought had major faults?
....

6 What type of kettle do you currently have? ......

7 Is it: Reliable □ Unreliable □ Average reliability □

8 Which of the following makes would you choose if price did not matter?

Swan Cool Touch Cordless □
Kenwood Cordless Automatic □
Russell Hobbs Country Style □
Tefal Freeline De Luxe □
Haden Automatic □

9 How many company names do you remember from advertising?

10 Is price an important consideration? Yes/No

11 How often do you use your kettle. Often/Sometimes/Hardly Ever.

12 What do you use your kettle for? ....

13 How did you pay for your last kettle? ....

14 Which in question 8 wouldn't you choose? ......

15 Who else has a kettle like yours? ....

16 Do they use it: Very often □ Hardly Ever □ Frequently □ Rarely □ Mainly at weekends □ Never □ Sometimes □

17 Are you: Upper Class □ Upper Middle Class □ Lower Middle Class □ Upper Working Class □ Lower Working Class □

Figure 3.4
What a mess!

too many questions. A question should only be included if it relates to your needs.

Questions can be open or closed. Open questions are those which allow the person answering to give an opinion and which encourage them to talk at length. Closed questions usually require a yes/no answer or one picked from a range of options. Questionnaires nearly always use closed questions. This tends to mean that the questions can be answered more quickly and more efficiently. It also means that, because the information is much more structured, the answers are easier to analyse: For example:

Do you find that the speed with which your kettle boils water is:

a

Very fast	Fast	Satisfactory	Slow	Very slow

(tick where appropriate)

b Very fast ☐☐☐☐☐ Very slow

tendency to
(tick where appropriate)

The purpose of this type of question should be to try and get people to commit themselves to a concrete opinion – in this example, their view as to the speed of their current kettle. If an open question had been asked the likelihood is that a variety of different answers would have resulted. Closed questions tie respondents down so that they have to make a decision within a range of choices (in this case a range from very fast to very slow.)

Closed questions for which you suggest a range of answers can make it easy to sort your answers for analysis, for example:

Which of the following methods of payment do you use most regularly? (Tick the relevant box)

Notes and coins ☐

Cheque payment ☐

Credit card ☐

Other means ☐

Sometimes, you will need to ask open questions. For example, if you wanted to find out why people are or happy or unhappy with the performance of their kettle, the range of answers you would have to provide might be too broad to be practical within a closed question. An open question will help you to discover people's real views about their kettle's performance and to communicate these views more effectively.

When designing your questionnaire you will need to give careful thought to how you can make sure that respondents concentrate on questions which are relevant to them, and skip over questions which do not relate to them. This will be important with questions which provide two or more possible answers, for example:

Question 1 Do you have a cordless kettle?
- Yes
- No

If your answer is no skip to question 12.

(Questions 2–11 would then be filled in only by those respondents with cordless kettles.)

Task

Set out a questionnaire with fifteen questions to find out what types of shops members of your class prefer to shop in for fashion clothes.

Set out the questionnaire so that some of the questions can be skipped over by certain respondents.

CASE STUDY

Setting out a questionnaire

A class of students set out to find if there was a demand for a second screen at their local cinema. They needed to find out the answers to questions such as how many people went to the cinema, how often they went, what sort of people they were and the types of films they liked.

This sort of information would show whether there was a large demand for a cinema, the type of people who would go most frequently, and what types of films would attract the biggest audiences.

The class had already been told by the cinema owner that age was a very important factor influencing the frequency with which people went to the cinema and the types of film they preferred to see.

The class then set out to classify cinema-goers into different age groups. First they took into account their own experiences and then interviewed friends and relatives in different age groups. Using this information they were able to come up with the following groups:

5–15	16–25	26–35	36–50	51+

Having chosen their main criterion for classification they were able to devise a questionnaire containing all the other questions they needed to ask. The questionnaire was simple to use in the field and easy to read off when completed.

A short section of the questionnaire is shown below:

	5–15	16–25	26–35	36–50	51+
How often do you go to the cinema?					
more than once a week once a week once a fortnight once a month hardly ever never					
What types of films do you mainly watch?	5–15	16–25	26–36	36–50	51+
Horror Adventure Comedy Romance					

Figure 3.5
The cinema questionnaire

Your market research questionnaire

Your task is to design a market research questionnaire to see if there is the demand for an additional screen at your local cinema. You should consider the following questions.

● What will you ask?

● Who will you ask?

● When will you ask?

● How will you ask?

Collect and record your information. Then, present a report on your findings and recommendations to your local cinema owner.

Alternatively you could research the demand for:

● a new supermarket ● a new car park

● a new leisure centre ● a new disco,

You will find it helpful to carry out a pilot survey to test your questions before you go for a full survey.

Sampling

Market research is used to chart consumer needs and wants. To achieve accurate information, every person within a defined population needs to be asked the same questions in the same way. If the selection of the sample is fair and accurate, then information about the defined population should be statistically reliable.

Surveys

Surveys are either **random** or **quota**. In both cases, the first step is to choose the districts or sampling points in which interviews will be carried out.

This will involve listing all possible areas and making a random selection, primarily taking into account region and population size, as well as structure.

Depending upon the survey, other stratification variables might also be included. These could cover political status or demographics for example.

For a random survey, individuals are pre-selected, from a **sampling frame** – the electoral register for example. The interviewer is required to make a number of calls at each selected household in order to make contact with the named individual. Most government surveys and some large commercial surveys are carried out by means of random sampling.

While random sampling is better from a theoretical point of view, it does tend to be more expensive and time-consuming, than the more commonly used research method of quota sampling.

When using the quota sampling method, the interviewer is given instructions as to the number of people to interview and their characteristics, defined in terms of sex, age or social class groups or other demographic detail.

The quotas will of course, reflect the fact that some members of the population are much more difficult to question – those who work full time or those in the younger age groups, for instance.

The sample size will determine the level of accuracy of the data. Figure 3.6 below illustrates the relationship between these variables for a random survey at 95% confidence levels (in other words that 19 out of 20 surveys will fall within the stated values).

Figure 3.6

Sample size	10% + or −	20% + or −	30% + or −	40% + or −	50% + or −
4000	0.9%	1.2%	1.4%	1.5%	1.5%
2000	1.3%	1.8%	2.0%	2.1%	2.2%
1000	2.0%	2.0%	3.0%	3.0%	3.0%
500	3.0%	4.0%	4.0%	4.0%	4.0%
200	4.0%	6.0%	6.0%	7.0%	7.0%
100	6.0%	8.0%	9.0%	10.0%	10.0%

Eg with a random sample size of 2000 an observed response of 30% indicates that the true figures will be between 28% and 32% (in other words 2% either way) in 95% of cases.

Limitations on collection of data

Several restraining influences should be placed on the collection of information as defined by the objective. Some are general influences such as the constraints, budgetary restrictions, and storage capacity. Other equally important limits are imposed by relevance.

Of the wealth of information held by various departments within the company, only some will have any value in marketing terms. It is important to be selective before data collection starts otherwise a great deal of time and effort will go into collating information that is never used or is not relevant.

The main areas of information gathering have been defined:

i   internal information concerning our own customers.

ii   external souces concerning the market and relevant products.

iii   information collected by research.

The most restrictive limitation on internal research is its relevance. It must also be easy to update. It is not therefore simply a matter of using information as it is presented but 'translating' it to tell us what we need to know. There are limitations on how much this information, which has been collected for another purpose, can be of value to a marketing function.

External sources present much the same problem in their sheer diversity, accessibility and usability. Again, before embarking on an investigative programme, the parameters must be clearly defined. This will help to ensure that any time, money and effort allocated to the research is well used.

The same rules must apply to research projects. The requirements should be carefully considered to ensure that the results provide valuable information concerning the relevant issues and market areas. The objectives will also usually dictate the technique adopted for conducting the research.

Cost/risk of research

The value of research should be defined by its objectives, how important and potentially valuable it is for the company to have that particular information.

If deemed to be of high value, it will more than likely justify higher expenditure.

There are many elements to costing market research which vary enormously according to the nature of the project. If a consultant or market research organisation is hired, costs will rise significantly. However, it is crucially important that cost-cutting does not affect the quality of the project undertaken as this can materially affect the results.

The most expensive market research techniques are group discussions, interviews and telephone surveys. However, a 100% response rate is generally guaranteed, and the information gathered can be very detailed and subjective in a way that a technique such as desk research cannot. However, desk research and postal surveys can provide comprehensive results for a quantitative study, and are therefore considered cost-effective for this kind of project.

The danger with all research is that the planning stage is neglected. If this is the case, however much money is spent on it the results will reflect the inadequate nature of the planning stage. It is crucial, therefore, that all aspects of the research are carefully planned and investigated, before implementation.

Application of researched data

Market research can be made to investigate many aspects of a business for different purposes. It is usual to start with the company, its products and services, its sales and its customers. This alone can give a valuable insight into the elements that go into determining the nature of a company.

However, to give this snapshot a background, market research can be used to tell you how your company stands within the industry, about your competitors, about the market and the opportunities it might offer, as well as threats it may present.

To paint the fullest picture of all national economic factors, social influences and government policies all need to be taken into account.

If starting afresh, this would be the order of priority when newly researching a company. What the company knows about itself and its customers is better than anyone else's information on the same subject, as it is the most relevant and accurate. This should be built upon from secondary sources to complete the picture.

The implementation of market research findings, unwelcome or otherwise, bring the research process towards a full circle. Having implemented them, a monitoring process should be put in place to measure improvements, and if the desired results from implementation are not achieved a further round of research may be required to establish the reasons.

Costs of marketing

It is important to remember that marketing is not a static process. The market needs to be constantly monitored, researched, and improvements made to the products and services on offer to the customers.

The costs of meeting the company's and the customers' requirements can vary but, by knowing as much as possible about the environment in which the company operates, effort can be made to ensure that the marketing budget is cost effectively applied by minimising wastage and targeting the marketing effort as precisely as possible. The budget must not just cover the research requirements but all elements of the marketing mix.

Depending on the nature of the market being addressed, the costs are generally higher the more specialist the market, therefore on a cost-per-thousand basis the C1, C2, female 45+ group is more difficult and therefore more expensive to identify than all adults.

It is well known however, that the more tightly the target market is identified, the better the response will be, and the more cost effective the expenditure.

Cost efficiency holds the key to effective marketing, and prioritising that expenditure is important to ensure that the maximum potential benefit receives more urgent attention than other issues, all of which is part of ensuring cost effective use of resources.

CHAPTER 4
The Marketing Mix

Matching objectives

Up to this stage we have looked at the areas of marketing that prepare for change or for any decision to be made. But marketing is not just about *preparation* it is also about *action*. It is the energy that drives our economy and is responsible for bringing goods and services that consumers need into the marketplace for the process of exchange to take place. In doing so, the behaviour of organisations will reflect their corporate objectives and this will in turn influence the strategies and techniques they develop. Such objectives provide organisations with a unifying purpose and also create a yardstick against which they can assess their achievements.

It is usually assumed that the purpose of all businesses is both to make and maximise profits but the modern business environment is more complex than ever before. The management team have to assume responsibility for the decisions they take because they influence shareholders, customers, employees, creditors and suppliers. No group has a more vital role in doing this than those involved in marketing.

The role of marketing management is to establish a plan which helps an organisation to achieve its objectives. From this plan decisions have to be made to turn ideas into reality. Such decisions will involve the ingredients of **The marketing mix**, all of which are capable of being creatively fashioned in order to generate the required progress.

Corporate planning

The first question that any organisation must ask itself is 'where are we going?' Apart from maximising profits, many search for brand leadership or market domination. By achieving such a position they feel that they have obtained stability and developed security.

Corporate growth is also a common objective. Taking over other companies, diversifying and introducing new products might not always help profitability but it will provide managers with control over a larger corporate unit. Many organisations are immensely proud of the way they are viewed by others. Some might be prepared to sacrifice profitability but never reputation.

At the heart of corporate planning lies the need to match marketing objectives with corporate objectives. Doing so directs an organisation's activities towards satisfying the wishes of the consumer and enables it to achieve its goals.

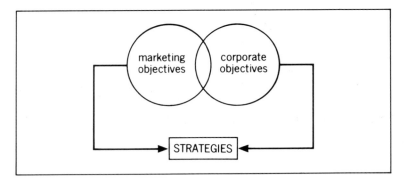

Figure 4.1
Matching objectives

CASE STUDY   **British Airways**

British Airways is not only the world's largest airline, but also one of the most profitable. It has always maintained a leading position in the world airline industry. For example, it operated the world's first daily scheduled international air service, the world's first jet passenger flight and the world's first commercial supersonic aircraft.

Today British Airways seeks to continue to set the trends that the rest of the industry follows. Its objective is to maintain corporate growth and to take advantage of the anticipated global expansion of the industry. To achieve this objective BA believes in the need to expand traditional markets by increasing activities in regional British cities and outside Britain.

As air travel becomes commoner and more frequent for many people, expectations grow. For those involved in marketing at British Airways, the objective is to provide better quality goods and services and good value for money in every market segment in which they operate as rivals seek to achieve a competitive edge. This will involve maintaining quality, innovation and service, whilst constantly responding to the requirements, preferences and aspirations of customers.

Figure 4.2
British Airways – setting the trends for the rest of the industry
(Source: British Airways)

Task 1
Look carefully at both the corporate and marketing objectives shown in the case study. Describe how achieving the marketing objective will enable British Airways to reach its corporate goal.

Task 2
Suggest three alternative courses of action which the British Airways marketing team could adopt to work towards their objective.

The marketing mix

The **marketing mix** comprises a complex mix of variables which an organisation can combine in order to ensure that marketing and corporate objectives are achieved. It will include strategic, tactical and operational elements and techniques.

It is usually analysed on the basis of the Four P's. To meet the customers needs an organisation must develop *products* to satisfy them, charge them the right *price*, get the goods to the right *place* and make the existence of the product known through its *promotion*.

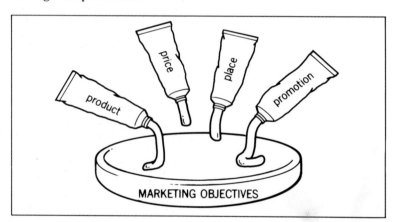

Figure 4.3
The Marketing Mix

'Mix' is an appropriate word to describe the marketing process. A mix is a composition of ingredients blended together to fulfil a common purpose. Every ingredient is vitally important and each depends upon the other for its contribution. Just as with a cake, each ingredient is not sufficient on its own but blended together it is possible to produce something very special. In the same way that there are a variety of cakes to suit various tastes, a marketing mix can be designed to suit the precise requirements of a market.

As a result the marketing mix must have:

●   a time-scale. An organisation must have a plan which indicates when it expects to achieve its objectives. Some objectives will be set to be attained in the near future. Others might be medium term (one to five years) and others might be visionary objectives for attainment in the longer term.

- strategic elements. These will involve the overall strategy of the organisation. They require considerable use of judgement and expertise and are only made by senior managers. Such decisions might involve the development of a new product or a new market strategy.

- tactical or medium term elements. The business environment has to be constantly monitored and decisions have to be taken according to whatever changes take place. External events might affect pricing strategies, product modifications or amendments to marketing plans.

- short term operational elements. These involve predictable everyday decisions such as contacts with customers, analysis of advertising copy and minor decisions about packaging.

The commitment and support of a programme of planning with sufficient resources will underlie the manipulation of the marketing mix and will ultimately determine how capable an organisation is of achieving its objectives.

CASE STUDY   Sony Video Walkman

Recently Sony launched its revolutionary Video Walkman, backed by its biggest corporate advertising campaign to date, which cost £10 million. The Video Walkman is a full-feature video recorder and television combined to make an item only slightly larger than a Filofax. Initially it will sell for £799, but a cheaper play-only version will be available once a market for tapes becomes established. Its 8mm format allows it to use videotapes the size of an audio cassette.

As part of the launch, Sony spent £1 million on buying 8mm software for the UK market. Initially these have been sold by retailers placing telephone orders with Sony — 'only to order' selling — but it is believed that when retailers see the growth, they will stock the films themselves.

Despite a price that will initially keep the product out of the mass market, Sony is confident of success, and expects to sell 15 000 units through retailers in its first year.

Task 1
Identify each of the four ingredients of the marketing mix illustrated in this case study.

Task 2
Comment upon how each of these ingredients might be varied in the future if Sony wanted to make the product appeal to the mass market.

The product

The product is the central point on which all marketing energies must converge. The product is more fully discussed in Chapter 5. Finding out how to make the product, setting up the production line, providing the finance and manufacturing the product are not the responsibility of the marketing department. However, they are concerned with what the product means to the customer. People buy goods and services for a variety of reasons and a wide range of characteristics will influence their decision to buy. These include:

- appearance – often the way a product looks is considered to be as important as what it can do. Carpets, furniture and jewellery are goods which must be designed to appeal to the tastes of the customer.

- function – consumers will want to know what a product can do and how well it can do it. When you buy a car you might want it to accelerate quickly or last a long time. The functions of a car which are necessary to a taxi driver may be radically different to the functions for a motorist who wishes to use the vehicle for recreational use.

- status – consumers often associate products with a particular lifestyle. Organisations often try to emphasize this association to create an image for the product. For example, certain car badges and designer labels encourage consumers to make the purchase because of the status they portray. Red Stripe, the premium lager brand marketed by HP Bulmer, was successful because of its cult status.

Figure 4.4
The 'Cult status' associated with Red Stripe
(Source: HP Bulmer Ltd)

The product range and how it is used is a function of the marketing mix. The range may be broadened or a brand may be extended for tactical reasons such as matching competition or catering for seasonal fluctuations. Alternatively, a product may be repositioned to make it more acceptable for a new group of consumers as part of a long term strategic plan.

The price

Of all the aspects of the marketing mix, price is the one which creates sales revenue – all of the others are costs. The price of an item is clearly an important determinant of the value of sales made (see Chapter 6.) In theory, price is really determined by the discovery of what customers perceive is the value of the item on sale. Researching consumer opinion about pricing is important as it indicates how they value what they are looking for as well as what they want to pay. An organisation's pricing policy will vary according to time and circumstances. Crudely speaking, the value of water in the Lake District will be considerably different to the value of water in a desert.

The place

Though figures vary widely from product to product, roughly a fifth of the cost of a product goes on getting it to the customer. The issue of 'place' deals with various methods of transporting and storing goods, and then making them available for the customer. Getting the right product to the right place at the right time involves the distribution system (see Chapter 7.) The choice of distribution method will depend upon a variety of circumstances. It will be more convenient for some manufacturers to sell to wholesalers who then sell to retailers, while others will prefer to sell directly to retailers or customers.

As the distribution system is constantly changing, organisations need to update their plans frequently. The type of distribution network chosen for each product should be compatible with other elements in the mix and will help to reinforce the overall nature of the marketing mix.

The promotion

Promotion is the business of communicating with customers. It will provide information that will assist them in making a decision to purchase a product or service (see Chapter 8.) The razzamatazz, pace and creativity of some promotional activities are almost alien to normal business activities.

The cost associated with promotion or advertising goods and services often represents a sizeable proportion of the overall cost of producing an item. However, successful promotion increases sales so that advertising and other costs are spread over a larger output. Though increased promotional activity is often a sign of a response to a problem such as competitive activity, it enables an organisation to develop and build up a succession of messages and can be extremely cost effective.

The importance of the mix

The marketing mix is a carefully constructed combination of techniques, resources and tactics which form the basis of a marketing plan geared to achieve and match both marketing and corporate objectives. Whenever objectives or external influences change, so the blend of ingredients will have to be varied. The effective solution to any problem will involve the careful scrutiny of every element. Changes to the mix have to be carefully considered and implications have to be assessed. Often timing is of crucial importance.

A ratio can be used to calculate the effectiveness of a change in a component in the mix and then relate it to its cost. A successful change would be one where the effectiveness-to-cost ratio is at its maximum.

No two mixes, even between similar types of organisations, will ever be the same. Each will represent a unique approach to developing a strategy for the resources they have available.

Choosing marketing strategies

Undifferentiated marketing exists where a single marketing mix is offered to the total market. This is unlikely to be successful because, as we have seen (in Chapter 2), markets consist of different types of buyers with different wants and needs.

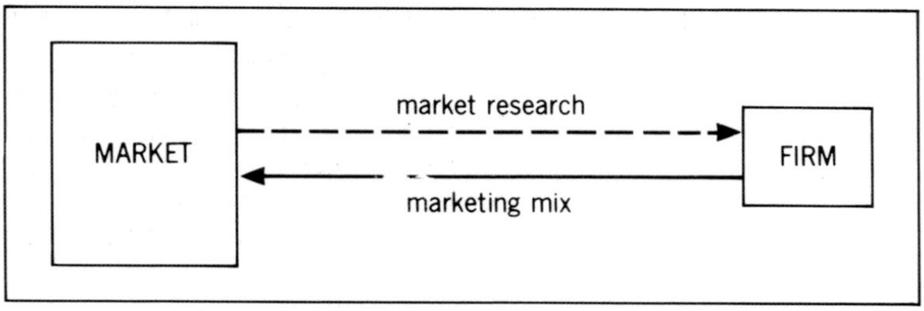

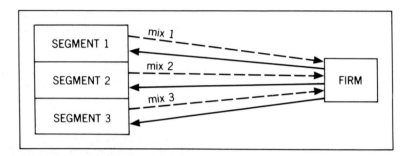

Figure 4.5
Undifferentiated marketing

Differentiated marketing is the strategy of attacking the market by tailoring separate product and marketing strategies to different sectors of the market. For example, the car market may be divided into an economy segment, a luxury segment, a performance segment, etc.

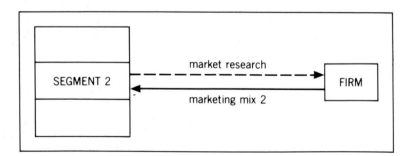

Figure 4.6
Differentiated marketing

Concentrated marketing is often the best strategy for the smaller firm. This involves choosing to compete in one segment and developing the most effective mix for this sub-market. Jaguar, for example, concentrates on the luxury segment of the car market.

Figure 4.7
Concentrated marketing

Although companies will try to select and dominate certain market segments, they will find that rivals are engaged in similar strategies. They will therefore try to create a differential advantage over rivals. The *positioning* strategy of a business relates to selecting a market segment and creating a **differential advantage** over rivals in that area. For example, Porsche is positioned in the prestige section of the car market with a differential advantage based upon technical performance.

CASE STUDY **'Ecologically sound' household products**

Recently the battle for the green consumer intensified with the unveiling of a campaign to promote public awareness of the dangers of conventional detergents as well as a new range of 'ecologically sound' household products. Both are important events in the 'soap war' between the new, up-and-coming green organisations and the traditional soap giants such as Lever and Proctor & Gamble.

The green campaign message is promoted by Belgian-owned cleaning products company **Ecover**, who hope to boost public awareness of the pollution problems caused by conventional detergents. Phosphates are used in UK-manufactured detergents but are banned in Switzerland, limited to 2% in Italy, and severely restricted in West Germany and Holland. Ecover has produced a 'Green Paper' entitled *Towards a cleaner and safer world*.

At the same time, **Ark**, the recently founded environmental group which, as part of its activities, markets environmentally responsible consumer products, launched its own range of household products. It includes washing-up liquid, lavatory cleaner, window cleaner, soap powder and liquid soap. Ark tries to ensure that its products are comparable or superior to leading brands in performance, that they are priced comparably, are mainstream in appearance and are also informative to the consumer.

Figure 4.8
Environmentally responsible
consumer products *(Source: Ark)*

Task 1
Comment briefly upon the nature of the market for soap and cleaning products.

● Describe the sort of marketing strategies adopted by Ecover and Ark. How do such strategies provide them with a differential advantage?

● Explain why it would be more difficult for the soap giants to attract the green consumer.

Managing change   Over a period of time, tastes, fashions and trends alter and the nature of technologies moves forward. No organisation can afford to sit back and enjoy their rewards without considering their next move. Competitive advantages are gained through becoming technologically advanced, innovative and unique in their approach to managing change. Those that fail do so for a variety of reasons. Some do not adapt products to meet the requirements of the market. Others do not anticipate the reactions of the competition and wake up to discover that their performances are not what they expected. Both of these affect the money coming into the business and one of the most frequent causes of business failure is an inability to forecast cashflow.

The components in the marketing mix are interdependent. For example, if a company is able to rely upon the distribution system and the distributors within it to sell its products (*place*), it need not have such a large salesforce (*promotion*). The customers' perception of the *product* will determine *price* and *promotion*, etc. Managing the marketing mix must take this interdependence into consideration. For example, an ill-judged promotional campaign might damage a product's image and affect its positioning in the market place.

Understanding the marketing mix is essential for a marketing manager so that the mix can be managed in the most effective way in order to achieve objectives.

To manage change successfully, an organisation will identify the key success factors in their own business and then use the marketing mix to emphasize them more effectively. In order to do this they need to base their strategies upon an understanding of both their customers' responses and their competitive advantages and then move quickly to invest in their future.

The life cycle of a product

Changes in the marketing environment dictate that there will always be demand for new products and, at the same time, old ones will lose favour. We can all think of goods that everyone wanted at one time but which have since gone out of fashion. The Rubik Cube was conceived, born and obsolete in little more than a year. Some products, however, have staying power: wood as a raw material for furniture has been with us for as long as we can remember and looks likely to stay for a long while yet.

The **product life cycle** is an essential mechanism for planning changes in marketing activities. The environment in which organisations operate is constantly changing. Just as a child is conceived, born into infancy and then develops towards maturity, the product travels down a similar path. The product life cycle recognises that products have a finite market life and charts their lifetime through various phases. The sales performance of any product introduced into the market will rise from nothing, reach a peak and, at some stage decline.

The life cycle can be broken down further into distinct stages. In the introductory phase, growth is slow and volume low because of limited awareness of its existence. Sales then rise rapidly during the period of growth. It is during this phase that unit profit tends to reach a maximum as increased volume enables the benefits of **economies of scale** to be realised. Economies of scale describes a situation where increased output leads to a decrease in average long-term costs. Towards the end of this phase, competitors enter the market to promote their own products which reduces the rate

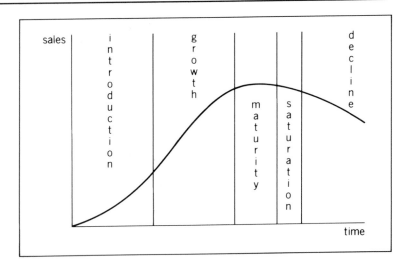

Figure 4.9
Stages in the Product Life Cycle

of growth of sales. This period is known as maturity. Competitive jockeying such as product differentiation in the form of flavours, colours, sizes, etc will sift out the weaker brands. During saturation, some brands will drop out of the market. The product market will eventually decline and it will reach a stage when it will become unprofitable.

The actual shape of any curve and the period of time it spends going through each of these stages will vary for each product or brand. They might depend upon market conditions, growth of particular market segments, or trends in buyer spending capacity. For example, high interest rates affect the DIY market. Technological developments also affect life cycles by providing for product improvements or rendering them obsolete.

Managing the life cycle

The life cycle may last for a few months or for hundreds of years. To prolong the life cycle of a brand or a product an organisation will need to readjust the ingredients of its marketing mix. Periodic injections of new life might include product improvements, line extensions or improved promotions.

A readjustment of the marketing mix might include:

● changing or modifying the *product* either to keep up with, or ahead of, competitors.

● altering distribution patterns to provide a more suitable *place* for the consumer to make purchases.

● changing *prices* to reflect competitive activities.

● considering carefully the style of *promotion*. Whereas in a product's early life the emphasis will be upon creating awareness, in the later stages it might be more appropriate to point out the advantages of the product over its competitors.

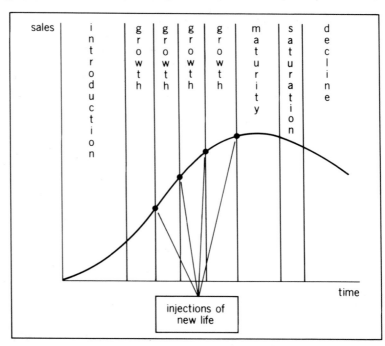

Figure 4.10
Periodic injections into the
product life cycle

CASE STUDY

Chambourcy shakes up its yoghurts

Chambourcy recently ditched its *Nouvelle* yoghurt brand in a major shake-up. The *Bonjour* name for set yoghurt will be relegated to pack corners as Chambourcy reclassifies its chilled range to:

- Le Yoghurt
- Le Fromage Frais
- Le Mousse
- Le Dessert
- and (for children) Hippo brands.

With increased advertising support emphasizing 'French-appeal' and packs carrying the name 'Chambourcy' in a prominent position, the strength of the brand will help them to improve their position in the market for yoghurts and chilled deserts.

The UK market for yoghurts and chilled deserts increased by a huge 110% between 1983 and 1987 and is forecast to rise a further 40% by 1992. Chambourcy has over 80 products in the chilled sector and feel that they can boost sales with improved signalling to the consumer to differentiate between various products on the market.

Task 1
What phase of their life have Chambourcy's products reached? Explain briefly how Chambourcy intends to increase its market share.

Task 2
Pick any brand which you regularly purchase or one that you can obtain the background of. Indicate where it falls in its product life cycle and show how periodic life has been injected into it.

Product portfolios

Most large companies produce a range of products, each of which has its own life cycle. By using life cycles, companies can plan when to introduce new lines as old products go into decline. The collection of products that a company produces is known as its product portfolio.

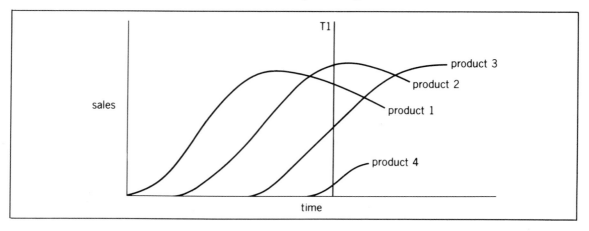

Figure 4.11
A product portfolio

In the above figure, T1 represents a point in time. At that point Product 1 is in decline, Product 2 is in maturity, Product 3 is in growth and Product 4 has recently been introduced.

If an organisation's products are becoming increasingly more appealing and are launched at just the right time, it will find that it benefits from a continuous period of steady growth.

Single product businesses are always likely to be vulnerable to variations in the market place. By spreading investment across a product range, an organisation reduces risks. Most businesses today are multi-product and provide a portfolio of products at different stages in their cycles. This helps to avoid serious fluctuations in profit levels and ensures that the most profitable products provide support for those which have not yet become quite so profitable.

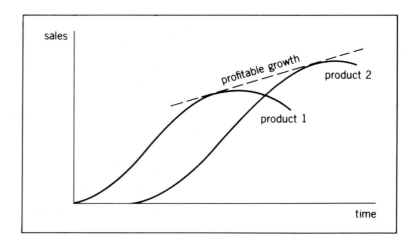

Figure 4.12
Growth

CASE STUDY   **Across the spectrum of Vauxhalls in the 1980s**

1980   Vauxhall Viceroy saloon arrives.
1981   New Vauxhall 'J' Cavalier launched.
1982   Diesel option for Vauxhall Astra and Cavalier.
         Cavalier 2-door convertible announced. The Astra Van
         introduced into the Bedford range.
1983   Vauxhall Nova and Astra GTE launched.
1984   All-new Astra range launched.
         Astra Van launched.
1985   Belmont models announced.
         UK sales of Vauxhall Cavalier reach half a million pounds.
         Astramax van announced.
1986   Vauxhall announces Astra convertible.
         New Carlton range introduced.
1987   Launch of the new Senator models.
         Nova GTE launched.
1988   Vauxhall-Lotus racing car announced.
         Launch of 16-valve Astra.
         All new Cavalier range introduced.
1989   Cavalier 4 × 4 available.
         Astra range grows to 32 models.
1990   Launch of Calibra.
         Restyled Nova.

The list shows the development of new Vauxhalls from 1980 to 1990. When you consider that, as with the Astra range, the number of models can grow up to and beyond 32 cars, that each product range is updated annually, and that there are a wide variety of colour choices in each product range, this gives you an idea of the massive scale of a product portfolio from a major car manufacturer.

Task 1
Look carefully at the timing of the product portfolio. What changes would you expect Vauxhall to make to its ranges in the 1990s?

Task 2
Examine the product portfolio of another major manufacturer. Comment upon timing, injections of life and the nature of their marketing mix.

Product life cycles provide a unique insight into the strategic implications for a group of products, and it can be argued that many mergers would not take place if organisations fully realised at what stage in their cycles the other organisations products were at. Governments might also refuse to provide aid if they thought that they were supporting declining products.

In practice, marketing is the selection of the optimum mix to support the objectives of the corporate plan. In the same way that the recipe provides a timing that is crucial to cooking, the product life cycle provides the marketer with an effective tool with which to predict events and manage the organisation.

CHAPTER 5

The Product

At some stage in their life most people come up with an idea for a new product. We have all met people with wild and wonderful ideas – 'a device for winding in electric fences on sheep farms', 'toothbrushes that play nursery rhymes when they are wet', 'automatic golf ball finders', and many more. None of these have ever gone beyond the stage of 'the idea' – yet!

Production involves going beyond the loose idea into market and product research to provide a marketable product. A product offers the purchaser a range of benefits. It will be composed of several elements.

On the surface there are often clear and tangible benefits – things you can touch and see. Tangible features of a product include:

- shape
- colour
- size
- design
- packaging.

The intangible features are not so obvious. These include the reputation of a firm – 'You can be sure of Shell', or the corporate or brand image – like the Shell logo.

There are extra features to be considered such as:

- after sales service
- availability of spare parts
- customer care policy
- guarantees.

What else can you think of?

A product is made up of a range of features which serve to meet customer requirements. A customer buying a new car may not just want a family saloon – additional requirements may be things like:

- a blue car
- four doors
- a well known name
- a long guarantee
- credit facilities
- after-sale free servicing
- low petrol consumption.

Product concept

At a simple level, a person buys a woolly jumper to keep warm. They buy an umbrella to keep dry in the rain, and a watch to tell them the time. However, as we have seen in previous chapters human buying behaviour is a complex process. It is not uncommon to hear someone say 'I wouldn't be seen dead wearing one of those'. In other words, for many of us, it can't be *any* old jumper, umbrella or watch! It needs to be an item that fits in with a particular perception or self image. Products are not usually purchased to meet a single need; the ownership and use of a product involves a whole range of factors that make up **product concept**.

For example, it may appear that a person chooses to holiday in the West Indies because they are attracted by the sand, sun and surf. However, when questioned further, it may come to light that they are more concerned with the 'image' which they present – friends, associates and other 'significant others' will become aware that they are able to afford to holiday in the West Indies. Holidaying in the West Indies is associated with a particular lifestyle. In the public imagination it may represent being rich and able to afford exotic things.

The purchaser of an expensive modern car will probably be interested in the quality and reliability of the vehicle. They may be attracted by the 'state of the art' technology and many other features of the car. However, a significant part of the product concept may also involve the ingredient of showing the world that 'they have arrived'.

In a similar way, you may like to purchase a second-hand trench coat from Oxfam not just because it will keep you warm and cost relatively little – in addition, you may believe that it gives you an 'arty image'.

Product dimensions

Product benefits can be broken down into a number of important dimensions. These include:

- generic dimensions
- sensual dimensions
- extended dimensions.

Generic dimensions are the key benefits of a particular item. Shoe polish cleans shoes. Freezers store frozen food. Deck chairs provide a comfortable seat on a sunny day. Hairdressers cut and style hair.

The **sensual dimensions** of a product are those that provide sensual benefits. These include design, colour, taste, smell and texture. A ring doughnut has a shape, appearance, texture, taste and smell all of its own. The sensual benefits of products are frequently highlighted by advertisers. This is clearly the case when advertising food and drinks – 'smooth and creamy', 'the amber nectar', and so on.

Extended dimensions of a product include a wide range of additional benefits. For example these will include servicing arrangements, credit facilities, guarantees, maintenance contracts and so on.

Research and development of products

Many people associate the research and development function of a company with the invention of new products. Whilst this is very important, the innovation and development of existing products is of equal significance. Consumer preferences are continually changing. The task of product research and development is to come up with the goods and services that will meet the needs of tomorrow's customers.

In any well-run company, research and development have strictly commercial functions – to further the company's business aims by creating better products, to improve operational processes and to provide expert advice to the rest of the company and to customers.

Some research cannot be expected to pay for itself within a foreseeable time span. Many large companies allocate a proportion of their research budgets, which may be as much as 5–10% in some cases, to so-called 'blue-sky' investigations which just may produce spectacular commercial results in the short term, but whose more likely contribution is to the long-term understanding of phenomena – with a possible pay-off in the far distant future.

Initially research and development must be related to an internal customer within a particular company. If you can't see a knowledgeable customer for research and development within your own organisation, the research and development process will be most unlikely to succeed.

Product research and development goes hand in hand with market research and development. Considerable liaison is required between these two areas, and processes need to be standardised. Setting up a production process or a new line can involve considerable cost, and careful work in the early stages will help to ensure that profits are made. Product researchers and marketing managers attempt to investigate all the questions indicated in figure 5.1 overleaf before a decision is made to finally go into production.

Task 1

You have come up with the idea of a mailbox which opens at the top, for the delivery of newspapers and post to households. The idea is that the box will be attached to the outside of front doors.

Now highlight areas of market and product research that will need to be covered before going into final production of the boxes at a factory unit. What are the key questions that you will need to consider? What are the key tasks that will need to be carried out?

Product researchers

Product researchers use marketing information to help them to develop products and choose suitable designs. Design is simply making things of quality that people want, products that range from toasters to machine tools that effectively carry out the job they are meant to do. The layout of a WHSmith bookshop for example, is an example of good design. A customer is able to

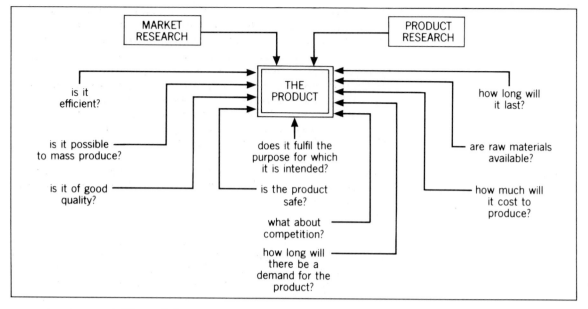

Figure 5.1
Key questions about the product

find quickly what he or she wants. The right use and allocation of space is vital to ensure profitability. So is the concept of service. WHSmith has been investing heavily in retail space and technology. In the late 1980s the company carried out a huge investment in point-of-sale data capture equipment.

Product researchers must also consider production costs, ease of manufacture and selling prices. A company might be reluctant to change an earlier design, particularly if it provides status, eg the radiator grill on a BMW car. Conversely, small changes may be made to products to bring them up-to-date. A company logo may be updated to give it a 'modern feel'.

Built-in obsolescence

Built-in obsolescence can, and frequently is, a feature of many products. Fashion clothes are designed to last for a season, and cars are built to last for only a few years. Manufacturers are able to sustain long term market demand by limiting the

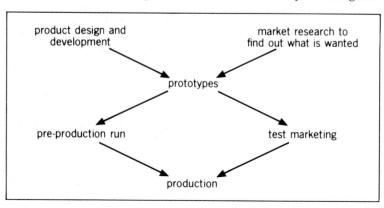

Figure 5.2
Stages in the production process

life span of a product. Some commentators argue that this leads to a huge waste of resources while others see it as boosting demand, employment and output in the economy.

Once a design has been developed the researchers will build a prototype which can then be tested. Many prototypes will be tried and then discarded while others may be modified and improved. Once a product has been tested and proved to be successful, and all the marketing and production questions have been answered, the firm will patent the product and will then consider 'tooling up' its production line.

Economic analysis of a product venture

An economic analysis of a production venture will need to take place as part of the process of research and development. The analysis will be based on estimations of future costs and revenues.

Cash flows

A large quantity of information related to outputs, prices, costs, taxes and royalties to be paid will need to be collated and assessed. When all this information is available for reliable estimates to be made, the annual net cash flow can be calculated. This is the total amount of cash coming into the company annually, based on expected volumes of product sales after allowing for the project expenditure.

The most uncertain assumption relates to the future product price. Some companies do not try to forecast the future price but assume instead a price profile that is prudent and realistic and test the economic viability of a project against that.

A typical example of an annual net cash flow is illustrated below. The positive cash movements of the venture should provide for the repayment of, and return on, the investment after taking into account the loss of purchasing power due to inflation.

The cash flow must produce a sufficient return in terms of the money of the day to offset this loss of purchasing power. To take account of likely future inflation, a real terms cash flow – expressed in money with a constant value – is calculated from the cash flow in money of the day (see figure 5.4)

The likely return on the investment, taking account of the risks inherent in the venture (and hence its economic acceptability), is examined by calculating a discounted cash flow. The risks are many and varied, and include technical and commercial risks, the risks of significant increases in technical costs, amongst other external factors (eg a change in tax structures).

It is extremely difficult to anticipate such possibilities in detail and, consequently, some companies prefer to test the economic acceptability of a project at a discount rate appropriate to an assumed level of risk. Such a discount rate is called the 'project screening rate' and usually ranges between 5–20%. A company is not completely free to choose what it feels to be an appropriate rate, since it must compete with others in the market.

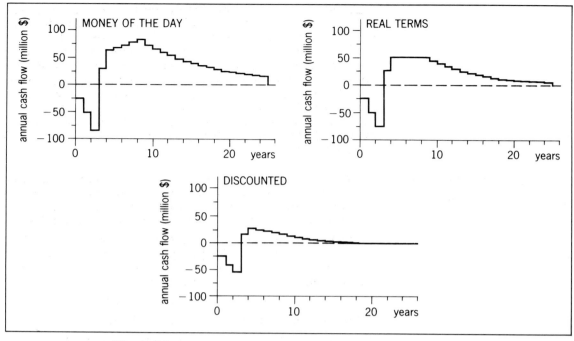

Figure 5.3
Annual cash flows

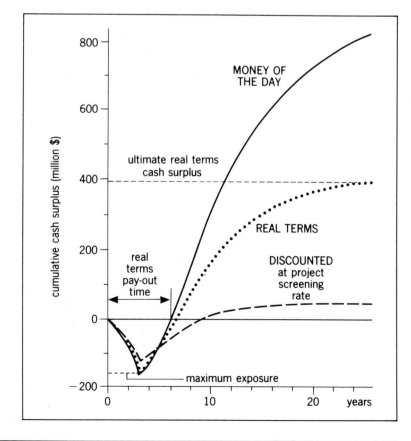

Figure 5.4
Cumulative cash flow

A useful way of understanding the future economic perform-ance of a project is the cumulative cash flow which is the progressive sum of the annual cash flow. An example is given in Fig 5.4. From this chart, a number of important measures of the economic acceptability of the venture are immediately apparent, such as the pay-out time, the maximum exposure and the ultimate cash surplus. The economic acceptability can now be judged according to the project's ability to meet the requirement that the cumulative cash surplus discounted at the project screening rate is positive and sufficient to justify the risks taken.

Forecasting product success

In Chapter 4 we looked at the life cycle of a product based on consumer demand. However, it is also important to look at restrictions imposed from the production side. We can illus-trate this point by looking at the exploration of oil fields.

Interest in an area may be triggered by a geologist's curiosity, a news item, or by an invitation from a government to bid for exploration rights. Before this can be developed further a realistic assessment must be made about:

- the probability of finding economic fields
- the contract terms that might be applicable
- economic aspects such as the production and transporta-tion costs.

These assessments are made to establish whether an explora-tion programme is justified, that is, whether anticipated benefits exceed expected costs.

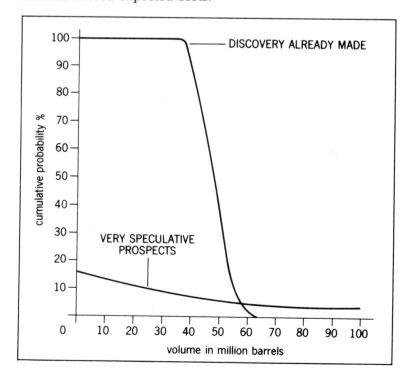

Figure 5.5
Expectation curves

An initial estimate of the reserves contained in a prospect can be expressed in the form of an expectation curve (see figure 5.5).

Expectation curves highlight the uncertainty associated with exploration (or any other form of production) – particularly at an early stage.

Based on an analysis of the geological information, expectation curves show the probabilities of finding reserves of a certain magnitude in the area. In a well defined area with a history of discoveries, for instance, there may be a high degree of certainty about the current reserves, but little chance of finding major additions. A speculative venture in a little known area, on the other hand, means that the chances of finding any hydrocarbons at all may be low – but there is an outside chance of making a very large discovery!

Task

Set out an expectation curve to show:

- small but certain prospects   ● poor, small prospects.

How can expectation curves be used as a management tool? As with all new major products developed by a large company, several steps of evaluation will take place before the final 'go ahead' is given.

Figure 5.6
A typical exploration programme

The activities involved in an exploration programme are aimed at defining the geological structures as accurately as possible as shown below.

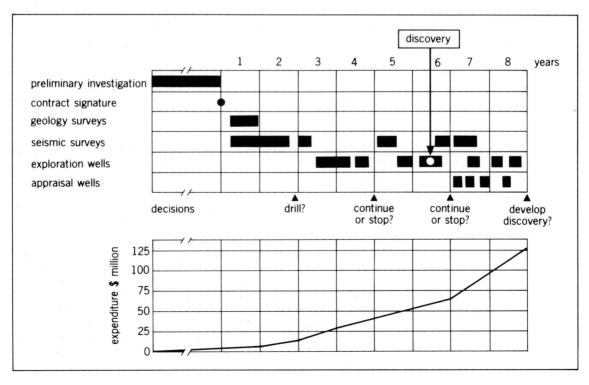

A preliminary investigation will identify whether there is a possibility of discovering oil. On the basis of this information contracts will be signed with the landowners to provide the basis for the right to develop the field. A geological survey will then be carried out, and periodic seismic studies will take place throughout the development stage. Exploration wells will be drilled to locate a point of extraction. Only after this has been done is it possible to determine whether oil and gas is trapped and whether the geological assumptions are valid. A cycle of further surveys and appraisal wells is undertaken to reduce the geological uncertainties and to provide an increasingly accurate estimate of oil and gas reserves.

Information obtained from these activities is used in planning the field development. With each cycle the costs of the exploration programme increase significantly. An efficient exploration programme is therefore one which obtains the maximum information with the minimum effort.

Product planning

In the exploitation of oil reserves, a given company will have a range of interests under review at any one moment in time. Some old fields will be drying up, others will be close to maturity, whilst newer fields will be flourishing, or still in the process of early development. Product planning involves devising methods to evaluate the performance of a portfolio of products, developing processes to extend the lives of some, to add bite to others, and planning the development of new initiatives. An oil company will usually have a wide range of interests including such things as gas and chemicals. The purpose of product planning is to make sure that you produce a mix which is compatible with company strategy.

The product mix

The product mix is the complete range of products produced by a company. Some business organisations try to diversify their range of products. By doing so they spread their risks over a wider field. In the last decade of the twentieth century we are seeing another trend amongst a number of large companies – they are simplifying operations to concentrate on their core strengths.

An example of a company that has diversified in recent years is WHSmith. On the high street, WHSmith dominates in four areas: books, stationery, magazines and 'sight and sound' (ie records, cassettes and videos). Selected stores also have travel agency departments. The 448-strong WHS chain is in itself insufficient to achieve this. Different kinds of retail outlets have had to be developed.

Currently there are 42 Sherratt and Hughes stores, appealing to the 20% of book buyers who consider WHS too down-market. There are also 172 Our Price record stores, attracting a younger age group. The latest development is the card, gift and stationery outfit, Paperchase, and the fifth element of the high-street mix is the growing chain of travel shops. Another area of WHSmith's activities is its out-of-town operation, the DIY retailer Do It All, which currently controls 8% of the DIY market.

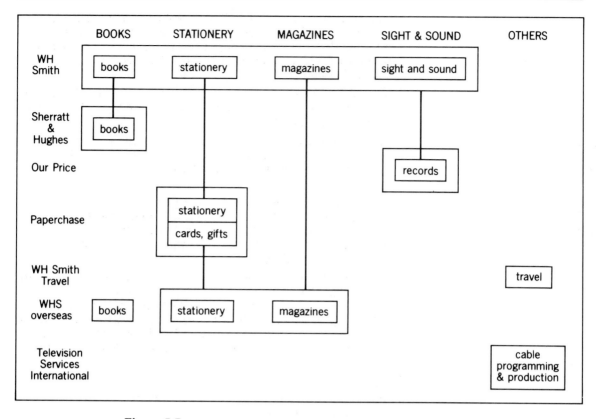

Figure 5.7
A diagramatic respresentation of
the WHS product mix

WHSmith is also a major wholesale distributor in the UK magazine and newspaper market.

WHS runs over 250 gift shops in the USA and claims to be Canada's biggest bookseller. Just to show its interests are not confined to the printed word plus a few records, WHS bought Television Services International in 1987 to gain an entry into the world of cable programming and production.

Task
Can you set out a chart to show the product mix of three well-known companies?

The key to a good product mix is having an effective balance of products in line with company strategy. Effective management involves creating this balance. If a product is losing its pulling power, it may need to be revamped, relaunched, or replaced.

CASE STUDY   Developing new products at SMH

Nicholas Hayek, Chairman and Chief Executive of SMH, the Swiss watchmaking firm, believes in beating the Japanese at their own game. The launch of the Swatch plastic watch in 1983 marked the start of the near-miraculous renaissance of the Swiss watchmaking industry, which had been laid waste by the Japanese.

Since then, nearly 70 million Swatch watches have been sold worldwide and Swatch has become the world's largest watch exporter. 'The Swatch message is simple – low cost, high quality, provocative and innovative design,' says Mr Hayek of his successful product.

SMH cut the number of parts in a normal watch from 150–250 to about 50 in the Swatch and devised new assembly methods that permit fully automated production.

Refined techniques helped boost sales of the group's medium and high priced watches, such as Omega, Longines and Tissot. 'If you lose the low market segment to the Japanese, you lose the rest,' asserts Mr Hayek.

Now he is trying other markets ripe for the Swatch formula – notably the European market for telephone equipment. Enter the Swatch Twinphone, a big seller in the United States since its launch last year and in Switzerland where it has been on sale since September 1989.

The Twinphone is aimed largely at the youth market, and is cheap (£30–£40), stylish (ten designs with names like Black Domino, Marsh Mallow and Limelight) and innovative. The Twinphone headset splits in two so that two people can speak simultaneously to a third. And it will memorise up to twenty numbers by name. Mr Hayek's ambitions do not stop there. His dream is a Swatch car!

Task 1

What do you understand by the following:

● 'innovative design'

● 'fully automated production'

● 'the volume market'?

Task 2

From information given in the extract, how would you describe the SMH marketing and product strategy?

Describe the changing product mix at SMH.

Why is product planning important to SMH? What does it involve?

CASE STUDY ## John Waddington's year up to 1990

John Waddington, the Leeds-based makers of Monopoly, Cluedo and Subbuteo, blamed weak markets in packaging and business forms for a 12.5% fall in pre-tax profits to £17.6m for the year to 31 March. The profit total was flattered by a £2.11m surplus on the sale of property and investments.

It also came before an extraordinary cost of £3.72m, due to the group's rationalisation programme, which included the closure of two operations, Ambassador Labels and Mono-Web.

The group's Bible printing operation, which also publishes Acts of Parliament, was bought in a management buyout operation in February.

Games, accounting for just over 10% of Waddington's turnover, bucked the trend for much of the toy industry, and profits rose 11% to £2.98m.

Packaging was hit by a move to more environment-friendly food packages. The business forms and specialist printing side was also hit by a downturn in the economy.

Waddingtons is refocussing its business forms operation to make more complex and specialised forms after a fall in demand.

Task 1
Explain the following:

● 'weak markets'

● 'rationalisation programme'

● 'management buyout'.

Task 2
What are the major elements of the product mix at Waddingtons? Do these elements complement each other? How?

Task 3
Explain how, and why, Waddingtons is finding it necessary to rationalise its operation. What will be the benefits of rationalisation

● for company organisation

● for future profits

● for the product mix?

Portfolio analysis

Perhaps the best-known method of analysing a product portfolio to see its balance was devised by the Boston Consultancy Group. The technique is based on the 'experience curve' which shows that the unit costs of adding value fall as cumulative production increases (see figure 5.9).

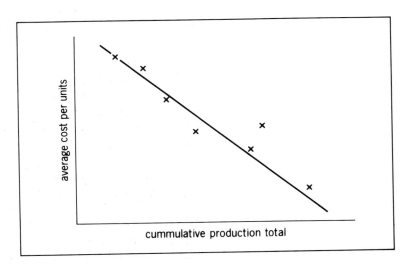

Figure 5.8
'Experience curve'

Gains in efficiency stem from greater experience. The Boston Consultancy Group argued that the principle had general currency and that as a rough rule, average cost per unit fell by 20–30% with each doubling of experience. Greater experience stems from:

- economies of scale
- the elimination of less efficient factors of production
- increased productivity stemming from technical changes and learning effects
- improvements in product design.

The importance of experience

The key lesson to be learnt is that the benefits of experience do not just arise – they need to be engineered. Companies must act to ensure that these benefits are reaped. They will result from active managerial policies.

An important implication of the work of the Boston Consultancy Group is that 'experience' is a key asset. Companies which have a high market share should be able to accumulate more experience. Therefore companies should strive for a high market share. The best indicator of market share is relative – that is, the ratio of a company's market share to that of its largest competitor.

Relative Market Share = Market share of Company A: Market share of nearest competitor

This indicator gives a clear measure of comparative strengths. The Boston Consultancy Group used statistical evidence to argue that a ratio of 2:1 would give a 20% cost advantage.

Product portfolio and market growth

The Boston Consultancy Group argued that the faster the growth of a particular market the greater the costs necessary to maintain market position. In a rapidly growing market, considerable expenditure will be required on investment in product lines, and to combat the threat posed by new firms and brands.

To summarise, the Boston Consultancy Group identified two key elements in the analysis of a product portfolio:

- The greater the cumulative experience the greater the cost advantage.
- The faster the growth of a market, the greater the cost of maintaining market position.

On the basis of these two general rules, BCG devised a portfolio matrix which is illustrated in figure 5.9 overleaf.

The matrix identifies four main types of products:

Prospects are those classes of products which compete in rapidly expanding markets. They take up large sums of cash for investment purposes. However, they also yield high cash returns. On balance they provide a neutral cash flow – but generally, they will go on to be the yielders of the future.

Yielders have a high market share in markets which are no longer rapidly expanding. Because the market is relatively

market growth \ relative market share	high	low
high	prospects	question marks
low	yielders	dogs

Figure 5.9
Product portfolio matrix

static they require few fresh injections of capital. Advertising and promotion will be required to inject fresh life from time to time. However, the net effect is of a positive cash flow. Yielders provide the bread and butter of a company in the form of profits at the end of the day.

Question marks have won a relatively low market share in fast growing markets. Can these be turned into market leaders? What needs to be done to improve their performance? These are just some of the key questions which will help to determine the viability of such products. The company knows that such products may go on to be powerful earners, but at the same time they may prove to be a drain on resources. What should be done with the question marks?

Dogs are products with a low market share in a low growing market. Because of the importance of experience these are products which are relatively poor competitors. As such they will generate a negative cash flow.

In terms of cash flow the product portfolio matrix can be redrawn in the following way:

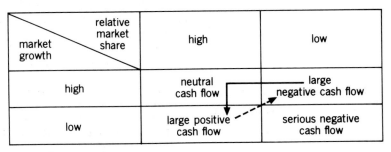

market growth \ relative market share	high	low
high	neutral cash flow	large negative cash flow
low	large positive cash flow	serious negative cash flow

Figure 5.10
A cash flow and product flow

product flow ⟶
cash flow ------➤

Cash generated by the yielders is used to help in the development of the question marks. The purpose of this is to increase the market share of the question marks in order to move them into the prospect category, with the expectation that they will eventually become yielders.

In order to manage the development of product success effectively it is important to have a balanced portfolio of products at any moment in time. A company will require a number of yielders to provide the bread and butter of the organisation (these are sometimes referred to as **cash cows**.) At the same time it is important to be developing the yielders of the future by investing in your prospects (or stars.) Fortunately the prospects will pay their own way. You therefore need to prop up your question marks and cut out your dogs.

Replacement/extension of existing products

What happens when a question mark fails to become a prospect? What happens when a yielder goes into decline? These are questions which require constant review by a marketing department. It is necessary to constantly re-evaluate the performance of products.

There are a number of ways of assessing performance.

1 Expected sales and profits. A product's performance can be evaluated against its previous performance. Once these indicators start to dip, there is a clear indication that remedial action needs to be taken.

2 Relative market share. Relative market share is always important because once it starts to fall the product becomes endangered by losing its competitive edge. Once it starts to lose impact in the public imagination it is in danger of being marginalised.

3 Threats. The development of threats in the market place need to be carefully monitored. Threats range from the development of new technology, the arrival of competition, changes in consumer expenditure patterns and so on.

Each product line within a company product portfolio claims a given share of scarce resources. As we saw in Chapter 1, these resources can be used in alternative ways – and there is an opportunity cost to be considered. If a product can be transformed from a declining position to one of high profitability then it will merit its position in the portfolio. If it is a drain on resources then it detracts from other products. At this time, it is important to prune weak areas, to replace declining products by new potential winners.

The launch of a new product

The launch is the most spectacular day in the life of a product (although the launch may spread over several weeks.) It is the time when a product is finally revealed to the critical scrutiny of the customer in the market place. In recent years the launching of products has become an art. At one time there was considerable secrecy associated with the launch. Today a common marketing technique is to provide sneak glimpses, and to provide leaked information to whet the appetite of the market. Previews and exposures to the press have become as common in marketing as in politics.

The major part of the advertising budget on a new product will normally be spent in the pre-launch and launch period. If the money invested in the launch is not to be wasted then it is important to blast off with dramatic effect. Champagne receptions for the press and chosen market contacts are standard practice in many consumer durable markets, coupled with extravagant sideshows.

For other consumer goods, expensive television and press advertising campaigns have become routine. Promotional pricing, trial offers, and free gifts are also effective ploys.

The launch should either make the potential market audience widely aware of the new product or make them want to find out more about the product. Whilst new product development is an important activity for companies, it is one that has a high degree of risk associated with it; hence, a large majority of new products that are launched either fail to be accepted by the market, or do not meet the financial criteria expected of them. One result is that a number of companies try to reduce the risks associated with product development, either by modifying existing products, or by copying competitors. Even with this latter strategy there is no guarantee of success. What is important is that market opportunities are studied carefully and related to the strengths and weaknesses of the firm.

A useful classification of new product development is based on the contrast between offensive and defensive. Offensive product development occurs with the application of new technology as well as responding positively to new patterns of consumer demand. Defensiveness is a reaction to competition in your area of business.

CASE STUDY

Toyota enters the executive car market (July 1990)

Toyota is attempting to coax executives away from their traditional Jaguars and BMWs with the British launch of its £34250 Lexus LS400.

The company hopes to repeat the four-litre car's success in the United States, where 24000 models have been sold since its introduction in September 1989. Toyota expects to sell only 600 of the cars in Britain in 1990, but is keen to break the European monopoly of executive saloons.

The Lexus
Powered by a V8 engine, the Lexus has gained a reputation for having 150mph performance without sacrificing quietness and a smooth ride. Features include anti-lock brakes, air-conditioning, leather upholstery and a compact disc player with seven speakers.

Toyota seems to have recognised that its biggest problem will be to create a separate identity for the Lexus in an expensive status-conscious market. Lexus, therefore, has a separate badge and the name Toyota does not appear on the car.

A special dealership network has been established among Toyota distributors, while a 'Club Lexus' warranty scheme, including hotel bills of £31.50 a night per person in the event of breakdown, is provided for three years.

Task 1
Identify the target market for the Lexus. What is the main competition in this market? How can this target market best be reached?

If you were responsible for launching the Lexus what steps would you take?

Task 2
In terms of the matrix developed by the Boston Consultancy Group, where would you place the Lexus in the Toyota portfolio? How can Toyota try to ensure that the Lexus performs well within the product portfolio?

What techniques have Toyota employed to ensure the success of the Lexus? Are these measures effective? What else needs to be done?

CASE STUDY **Chocolate Delight**

Chocolate Delight is a company that makes chocolates sold mainly in the South of England. The company has recently developed a new chocolate bar called PowerBar which is designed to appeal to children in the 8–13 age range. Chocolate Delight has installed a new production line which will only make PowerBars.

The company is hoping to sell the product widely in the Southern Television Area and will shortly make a decision on whether or not to spend £10000 on a television advertising campaign.

Chocolate Delight's sales department have estimated that with a television advertising campaign they will be able to sell 600000 bars a year at 20p each. Without television they would only sell 400000 at 20p.

Estimated costs for producing 600,000 bars (excluding television advertising) are:

wages	£50000
raw materials	£28000
repayment on loan to purchase new production line	£8000
other costs	£7500
	£93500

Estimated costs for producing 400000 bars are:

wages	£40000
raw materials	£20000
repayment on loan to purchase new production line	£8000
other costs	£7000
	£75000

Task 1

Why would television advertising be an effective way of promoting a new product? What is the estimated cost of producing

- 400 000 PowerBars?
- 600 000 PowerBars?

Task 2

What is the estimated revenue from selling

- 400 000 PowerBars?
- 600 000 PowerBars?

Task 3

Advise Chocolate Delight on whether it should go ahead with the proposed advertising campaign. Why might the actual costs and revenue figures for PowerBars turn out to be different from the estimated figures?

Chocolate Delight also produces small boxes of wafer-thin chocolate mints which they aim to sell to older, more affluent customers in the South of England.

Chocolate Delight's advertising department is hoping to spend £8 000 on advertising the product over a three month period by using at least two different advertising media. The cost of advertising using different media is shown below:

Cost of advertising

		£	
1	Television (Southern)	600	for 30 seconds off peak
		3 000	for 30 seconds on peak
2	Local radio	60	for a 30 second spot
3	National press	5 000	per insertion
4	Local press	500	per insertion
5	Free trade press	200	per insertion
6	Direct mailing		
	a. Post Office delivery	150	per thousand
	b. Hand delivery	20	per thousand
7	Posters (bus sides, advertising boards)	500	per poster
8	Leaflets	250	per thousand

Task 4

Given the advertising budget of £8 000 over a 3-month period and the chosen target group, advise Chocolate Delight which methods of advertising to adopt. Write a letter to the Marketing Director setting out your aims and evidence to support them.

CHAPTER

6 Pricing

The illustration below (figure 6.1) shows the price split at the pumps for a gallon of four star petrol. It brings home the fact that even a large company has only a limited degree of control over the price it can charge in the market. Costs of raw materials and production are important ingredients of price. So too are taxes to be paid, prices set by competitors, demand and supply conditions in the market, international geopolitical considerations (for example, the Gulf War) and exchange rates.

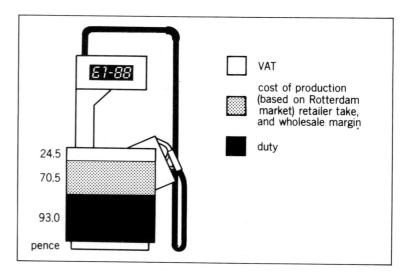

Figure 6.1
The breakdown of petrol
prices

Task 1
What is the current price of a gallon of four star petrol at your local service station?

Task 2
What factors could possibly have led to the change in the price of a gallon since late 1990, when figure 6.1 was set out? How many of these factors are within the control of petrol companies?

Defining price

The Oxford English Dictionary defines price as the **'sum or consideration or sacrifice for which a thing may be bought or attained.'**

However, to produce a watertight definition of pricing which gives a clear indication of its importance in the marketing mix is like trying to define the length of a piece of string. In some contexts, a particular definition will be appropriate, in others it will not.

A major problem stems from the fact that 'price' has different meanings for different groups of people:

Buyers price may be regarded to be an unwelcome cost. Price involves sacrificing the next best alternative that could be bought (this is sometimes referred to as opportunity cost). Price can also be used as a measure of the value of a particular item.

Sellers price is a key element in the marketing mix. It is an important selling point. Getting the 'price right' is an important tactical decision and as such it is a key factor influencing revenue and profit. We all know of a business that sold wonderful products, but which were just a little too expensive – it went bust. We also know of businesses which sold themselves too cheaply – not enough revenue was generated to cover costs adequately.

Government the price of individual products is an influence on the general price level – and hence votes!

These viewpoints about the nature of prices often conflict but they all need to be borne in mind when setting prices.

How important is price in the marketing mix?

The importance of price within the marketing mix varies from one market to another and between different segments in the same market. In low cost, non-fashion markets, price can be critical (for example in the sale of white emulsion and gloss paint for decorating). In fashion markets, such as fashion clothing, it can be one of the least relevant factors. Certain products are designed to suit a particular price segment (eg economy family cars) whilst others perform a specific function regardless of cost (eg sports cars). For consumers with limited budgets, price is a key purchasing criterion, whilst for others for whom 'money is no object', price is less important.

Pricing decisions

A number of situations can be identified in which pricing decisions have to be made. The most important of these include:

● when a price needs to be set for the first time. For example, when a new product is launched on the market, when new outlets are used, or when new contracts are made.

● When it becomes necessary to make a change in pricing structure. This may be because of the development of competition, a movement along the product life cycle, a change in demand or cost conditions.

What steps should a firm take in selecting an appropriate price in one of these situations? The firm will need to consider objectives, strategies and techniques.

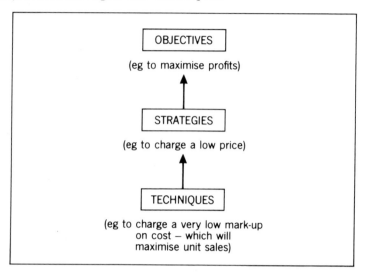

Figure 6.2
Objectives, strategies and techniques

Pricing objectives

The starting point in pricing should be to be clear about your goal or objective. Some possible objectives are:

Profit maximisation

A key assumption of many business theories is that profit maximisation is the most important pricing target. While it is true that unless businesses can make profits in the long run their futures will be uncertain, studies of actual business behaviour reveal a wide range of other objectives to short-term profit maximisation.

Price competition

A competitive price is one that gives a competitive edge in the market place. It is not necessarily one that is lower than that of a rival because other elements of the marketing mix add to the competitive edge. For example, it is possible to argue that Gillette razor blades are better quality than those of rivals, giving scope to charge a higher yet more competitive price than those applying to other blades.

A further element of competitive pricing is to set a price that deters new entrants in a particular market. Large firms with some degree of monopoly power may be inclined to keep prices relatively low in order to secure their long term market dominance. From time to time in business you will hear the owner of a small company say: 'Of course we would like to diversify into producing x but we simply couldn't compete with the prices being offered by the big boys.'

Yield on investment

Any money that is allocated to a particular use bears an opportunity cost. Could this money be spent in a better way? What are the alternatives that are sacrificed? Investors usually have expectations of what they regard to be an appropriate rate of return on investment. This yield will then be an important factor in determining pricing decisions. Investors will quickly make their feelings known to managers if they feel that the wrong pricing decisions are being made.

'Satisficing'

H.A. Simon put forward the view that businesses might want to 'satisfice', that is to achieve given targets for market share and profits from sales which may not maximise profits but would instead inflate boardroom egos. This can arise when the managers of a company are clearly different from the owners. If the managers can provide sufficient profits to keep the shareholders satisfied, then a proportion of profits can be diverted to provide more perks for managers and larger departments.

'Satisficing' policies are most likely to be associated with industries where there is only a limited degree of competition. 'Satisficing' objectives are fairly common in many organisations ranging from schools to oil companies. Managers will readily produce long lists of achievement which do not always relate to a profit margin at the bottom line. In large organisations it is often difficult to relate activities to financial statistics and managers with the ability to make a lot of noise can give the impression of being effective.

Other objectives

There are many other possible objectives in establishing prices. For example, a company may feel that it is important to maximise sales to create brand leadership, or it may want to establish a high price in order to establish a reputation for quality.

In setting the objectives outlined above, it is essential to remember that it is not only customers that may respond unfavourably. Other groups that need to be considered include:

- **competitors** who may choose to match price cuts, or not to match price increases.

- **distributors** who may insist on high margins and thus resist price cutting.

- **employees** who may ask for wage increases. (Wages are frequently one of the most important component costs).

- **Government bodies** who may withhold contracts, certificates or grants.

- **shareholders** by seeking higher dividends.

Pricing strategies

Once a pricing objective has been established, it is necessary to establish an appropriate strategy. Three broad pricing strategies can be considered.

Low price strategy

A low price strategy should be considered when consumers respond very positively to small downward changes in price.

In technical terms we can measure this response by means of calculating **elasticity of demand**. Elasticity of demand is the measure of changes in quantities purchased as a response to price changes. Demand is said to be elastic if the change in quantity demanded is of a greater proportion than the change in price that initiated it. If the price of a particular brand of washing powder fell by 10% and there was an increase in sales of 20% then the demand for the product would be said to be elastic. The change in price led to a more than proportionate response in quantity demanded.

Price elasticity of demand can be measured by the formula:

$$\frac{\% \text{ change in quantity demanded of product A}}{\% \text{ change in price of product A.}}$$

In our example $\frac{20\% \text{ (change in sales of washing powder)}}{10\% \text{ (change in price)}}$

$= 2.$

Products with a value greater than 1 are said to be elastic. However, it needs to be remembered that elastic demand does not always mean that a firm will benefit from price reductions. If a firm in a price sensitive market lowers its price, then there will be a strong chance that other competing firms will follow suit. Another consideration is cost. If a firm lowers price, and sells more, it may also have to pay out more in expenses and other costs.

A low pricing strategy is also important when it is easy to compare competitive products. For example, when brands of similar washing power sit side by side on the shelves of a supermarket there will be a strong incentive to charge a low price.

This is also true when the product cannot be classed as a necessity. Necessities tend to have low price elasticities when compared with luxury items. It is therefore possible to charge a relatively higher price for necessities in the knowledge that the consumer 'needs' to buy the product.

When the product is in plentiful supply it would also be a mistake to charge a high price – because the product is readily available.

In the situations outlined above, in which price cuts may lead to large increases in turnover, then a low price strategy may well strengthen a company's position, for example when selling to supermarket customers. Price in these situations plays a crucial role in the marketing mix.

Market price strategy

There are situations where one or more of the following conditions exist:

- products are bought frequently
- competitive products are highly similar
- a few large companies dominate supply in a specific industry.

In any of these situations, firms could quickly lose all their business if they set prices above the competition. Conversely, if they lower prices their competitors are forced to follow. Firms tend to set prices at market price level and the role of price is therefore *neutral*.

High price strategy

This can either be a long term or short term policy. A long term policy will mean that the firm seeks to sell a high quality product to a select market. High prices are an essential feature of up-market products. It is essential to maintain an exclusive image, to be reflected by the price. A short term policy is based on advantages gained by a patented product, a heavy investment in new equipment, or some other form of barrier to entry to a market.

In these circumstances price has a *negative* role in the marketing mix. When an appropriate strategy has been determined a suitable pricing technique can be chosen.

Pricing techniques

How are prices set in practice? Important influences on pricing techniques include:

- cost
- demand
- competitor's prices.

Practical pricing involves elements of all three. Below we explore some commonly used pricing techniques.

Cost-plus pricing

Any study of how firms price products in the real world inevitably reveals a very high proportion of businesses using no other basis than a mark-up on the cost of providing the product or service concerned. Information about costs is usually easier to piece together than information about other variables such as likely revenue. Firms will often therefore simply add a margin to unit cost. (The unit cost is the average cost of each item produced; if a firm produces 800 units at a total cost of £24 000 the unit cost will be £30.) Talk to many small business owners and they will tell you that they cost out each hour worked and then add a margin for profits, or they will simply mark up each item sold by a given percentage. For example, fashion clothes are frequently marked up by between 100 and 200%.

The process of cost-plus pricing can best be illustrated in relation to large firms where economies of scale can be spread over a considerable range of output. For a large firm, unit costs will fall rapidly at first as the overheads of a firm are spread over a larger output. Unit cost then becomes relatively stable over a considerable quantity of output. It is therefore a relatively simple calculation to add a fixed margin, eg 20% to unit cost. The firm is therefore able to select an output to produce and to set a price that will be 20% higher than the unit costs of production (see figure 6.3). Whilst cost-plus pricing is very popular, there are many dangers associated with it. If the price is too high, sales may fall short of expectations and if the price is set too low then potential revenue is sacrificed.

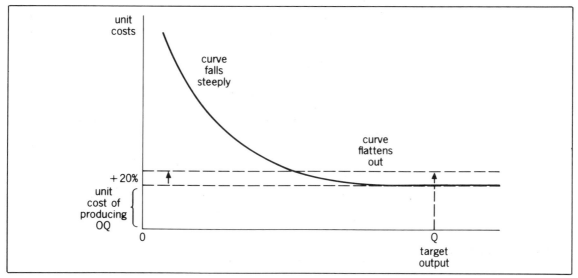

Figure 6.3
Select a target output OQ then add 20% to unit cost

The greatest danger of cost-based pricing is that it indicates a production-orientated approach to the market. Emphasis on costs leads to tunnel vision that looks inwards at the company's product rather than outwards to the customers' perception of the product.

If a firm applies unit cost-pricing too rigidly this can cause problems in the market-place. If demand is lower than expected, for example, unit costs may be slightly higher. In this situation the company accountant may press for price increases. This will make it even more difficult to make sales. If on the other hand, demand is higher than expected unit costs may fall slightly, demanding a price reduction. This may lead to a loss of potential revenue.

Contribution pricing

Contribution pricing involves separating out the different products that make up a company's portfolio, in order to charge individual prices appropriate to a product's share in total costs.

Two broad categories of costs can be identified:

Direct costs   vary directly with the quantity of output produced. For example, this may include costs of material used, wages to labour, and other expenses.

Indirect costs are costs that have to be paid, irrespective of the level of output. These may include the salaries of permanent staff, the cost of maintaining a plant and so on.

When a firm produces a range of individual items or products it is easy to determine direct costs, but not indirect costs. For example, in a food processing plant producing 100 different recipe dishes it is easy to work out how much goes on each line in terms of raw materials, labour input, and other direct costs. However, the same process cannot be applied to indirect costs – the salary of the managing director, the rates paid on the factory building and so on.

Contribution is the sum remaining after the direct costs of producing individual products have been subtracted from revenues.

When the contributions of all the individual products that a firm produces have been added together they should more than cover the firm's indirect costs.

There are strong arguments in favour of contribution pricing because of the way it separates out individual products and analyses them in terms of their ability to cover the direct costs which can be attributed to them. A new product may be brought 'on stream' because it can be shown that it will cover its direct costs and make a contribution to covering the company's total indirect costs.

In contrast, if we were to analyse individual products in terms of the relationship between their total revenue and total costs, calculations might show a loss. For example, if two products used the same distribution facilities, it would not make sense to expect both products to cover their own distribution costs individually. Contribution pricing enables a more rational analysis of individual products. Prices can be set in relation to each product's own direct costs (see figure 6.4).

Figure 6.4
Calculating profits

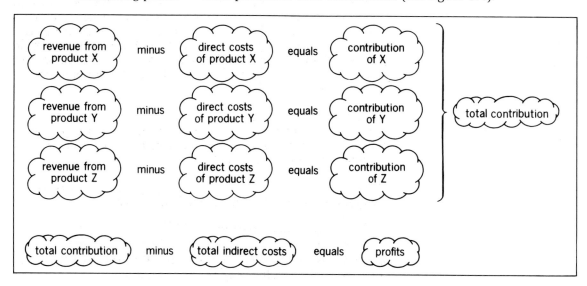

However, whilst contribution pricing is possible in many situations it is not so easy in others.

We can illustrate this by using the example of oil-based products. Oil product prices are set by a variety of market and other influences, both national and international, therefore, crude oil costs are only one element. Any cost allocated to a specific product must, by the nature of the production process, be an arbitrary one. This is because a barrel of crude oil is refined to produce the full range of petroleum products required by consumers, in varying quantities depending on the nature of the crude, the refining processes employed, and the pattern of demand at the time (see figure 6.5).

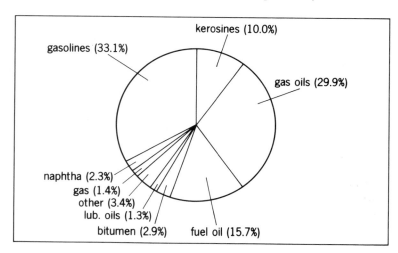

Figure 6.5
The barrel split from a typical UK refinery. Gasoline makes up about a third of the range of products refined per barrel

As with a butcher, who produces many different cuts of meat from one animal, there is no way, other than arbitrary choice, of establishing what share of the raw materials costs should be allocated to the product. It is competition in the market-place which establishes what the butcher can charge for each of his cuts of meat, and which sets the prices an oil company can obtain for its products. The company's objective is that these prices will add up to more than its overall costs and produce a profit for its shareholders that provides an adequate return on their investment.

Task 1
List five product areas in which contribution pricing may be easy to carry out. List five product areas in which contribution pricing may not be practical.

Task 2
Explain why in each case contribution pricing is

● possible

● impractical.

In each case of contribution pricing describe an alternative form of pricing which may be more suitable.

Demand-orientated pricing

Market research is essential to establish and monitor consumers' perceptions of price. Demand-orientated pricing involves reacting to the intensity of demand for a product, so that high demand leads to high prices and weak demand to low prices even though unit costs are similar.

When a firm can split up the market in which it operates into different sections, it can carry out a policy of price discrimination. This involves selling at high prices in sections of the market where demand is intense (where price is inelastic), and at relatively low prices where demand is elastic where there is a more than proportionate response in quantity demanded as a result of a fall in price. Price discrimination can be carried out in a number of situations.

Customer-orientated some customers may have an intense demand for a product while others only have a weak demand. Discrimination would involve selling the same type of product to the first type of customer at a high price and the second at a lower price. However, you can only do this if you can physically divide up your market so that the customer with the intense demand can not get hold of the lower-priced item. It is common practice to introduce some products at a higher price and then later to reduce the price. For example, many books are initially sold in hardback at a high price. When that segment of customers has been satisfied the cheaper paperback is published.

Product-orientated slight modifications can be made to a product to allow high and low price strategies. For example, many car models have additional extras – the two- or the four-door version, with or without sunroof, etc. Customers have the choice of the cheaper or more expensive version. In a similar way, you can purchase cheaper or more expensive versions of the same sewing machine, depending on whether you are prepared to pay for the additional facilities associated with the more expensive version.

Time-orientated sellers are able to discriminate when demand varies by season or time of day. In high season, a product can be sold at a high price. At other times, prices will need to be reduced. This applies to a wide range of items from fashion clothes to river cruises. Some products experience varying intensities of demand during the course of a single day – for example, telephone calls are charged at a much higher rate during the peak hours of the working day.

Situation-orientated this applies to houses – the same type of house may sell for one price in the centre of town and another price in a quiet suburban area. House prices vary widely from one area to another (eg the North-South divide). Cinema and theatre seats are also priced according to proximity to the screen or stage. Although production costs are similar, demand varies with situation. Price discrimination frequently takes place between countries. Different countries experience different average incomes and other factors influencing demand. Products will therefore be sold at different prices according to elasticities of demand in different countries, and regions within a country. For example, cars are much cheaper in Canada than they are in the UK.

Task 1
British Telecom uses discriminatory pricing according to time. Find out in detail how BT currently applies this policy. List and explain examples of other forms of price discrimination according to: customer, product version, time, and position.

Figure 6.6
British Telecom uses price discrimination according to time

In general, customers have views about what constitutes value for money. If prices are too high, they might not consider that they are getting value for money. If prices are too low, they will begin to question the quality of a product. A product would immediately lose its 'up-market' image if it was felt to be sold at a 'low price'.

From the consumers' point of view, value for money is a key ingredient when weighing up prices. Research carried out by *Marketing* magazine in the summer of 1990 on over 800 shoppers confirmed this view. They were able to argue that superior value in a store will overcome disadvantages in location, to some degree. Indeed, Asda, with a number of successful stores in not very visible or accessible sites, has proved that customers will beat a longer path to a superior outlet.

Reasons for choosing where to shop varied by region, with Southerners giving more weight to 'quality' in the value equation. Northerners rated their reasons like this:

1 prices/value for money

2 nearest to home

3 variety of goods

4 convenient/handy

5 know lay-out.

Southerners' ratings were slightly different:

1 prices/value for money

2 easy parking

3 convenient/handy

4 good quality products

5 know lay-out.

Low prices/value for money was the outstanding reason for choice of store. Other questions in the research confirmed that consumers carefully weighed price versus quality, in reaching a value judgement. Only a minority bought on price alone – 9% 'always checked and chose the cheapest', and 13% 'always bought things on special offer' even if they were not needed on that occasion.

By monitoring customer perceptions of price, a seller realises that the appropriate price band for a sale is in fact fairly limited (see figure 6.7).

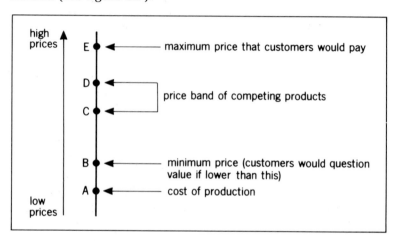

Figure 6.7
Customer perception of price

Let's assume that the product costs £A to produce. The business cannot sell the product for less than £B without its quality being questioned (how can it be sold for such a low price? is there something wrong with it?) Competing products are selling for prices between £C and £D, and the maximum chargeable price would be £E.

If the product is 'nothing special' in terms of customer perception then the price should be pitched between £B and £D. However, if the product is really exciting, and captures the imagination of consumers, it can be pitched anywhere between £C and £E.

Competition-orientated pricing

In extremely competitive situations, costs have to be ignored in short-term price determination. This is particularly true when competing products are almost identical, customers are well informed and there are few suppliers.

The nature and extent of competition is frequently an important influence on price. If a product is faced by direct competition, then it will compete against other highly similar products in the market place. This will often constrain pricing decisions so that price setting will need to be kept closely in line with rivals' actions. In contrast, when a product is faced by indirect competition (ie competition with products in different sectors of the market) then there will be more scope to vary price. This opens up the possibility for a number of strategies. For example, a firm might choose a high price strategy to give a product a 'quality' feel. In contrast, it might charge a low price so that consumers see the product as a 'bargain'.

An individual firm might try to insulate itself against price sensitivity by differentiating its products from those of rivals. Markets are sometimes classified according to the level of competition that applies. An extreme level of competition is termed **perfect competition** (it exists in theory rather than practice). The other extreme is **monopoly** where a single firm dominates a market. In the real world, most markets lie between these extremes and involve some level of imperfection.

---

perfect competition → imperfect competition → monopoly.

decreasing levels of competition

In a perfect market there would be no limitations to new firms entering a market, buyers would know exactly what was on offer, and incur no costs in buying from one seller rather than another. Products would be almost identical.

In a monopoly situation, only one firm would exist and barriers would prevent new firms from entering the market (eg a very high cost of setting up, the existence of patent and copyright restrictions and other barriers.) The seller would have considerable powers.

In imperfect markets as we know them, there may be few or many sellers. Products would however be differentiated and consumers would not have perfect information about the difference between products.

In the real world, businesses strive to give themselves the protection of monopolistic powers. They seek to reduce competition, and they seek to make their products seem 'better' than those offered by rivals. Monopolistic powers enable firms to push up prices and hence make larger profits. However, larger profits should not always be viewed as a cost to consumers. Profits can be ploughed into research and development, to advanced technology and the production of large outputs at lower average costs.

The level of competition should thus be seen as a key determinant of price.

In a situation where very close competition exists and products are virtually identical, there is almost no scope to charge a price which is different to those of competitors. This is as true of a situation where there are only two firms in the market (a duopoly) as when there are hundreds.

In a situation where there is no competition, the seller has considerable ability to charge a relatively high price. However, the seller cannot charge more than the consumer is prepared to pay. At the end of the day the consumers can spend their income on alternative products. Of course when goods are essential then the seller has more power, eg energy and food sales.

Between these two extremes, we find hundreds of different markets. In some the consumer has more power, in others the seller. It all depends on how easily supply can be altered in response to demand, and how demand is influenced by price.

Short term pricing policies

Pricing can be used as an incisive tool to pursue short term marketing and selling targets for a company. Typical attack-based policies include:

● Skimming pricing

● penetration pricing

● destroyer pricing

● promotional pricing

Skimming pricing

At the launch of a new product, there will frequently be little competition in the market, so that demand for the product may be relatively inelastic. Consumers will have little knowledge of the product. **Skimming** involves setting a relatively high initial price in order to yield high initial returns from those consumers willing to buy the new product. Once the first group of customers has been satisfied, the seller can then lower prices in order to make sales to new groups of customers. This process can be continued until a large section of the total market has been catered for. By operating in this way the business removes the risk of underpricing the product.

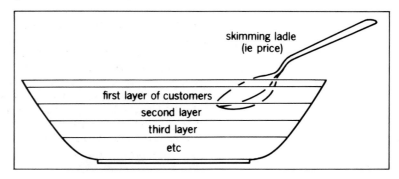

Figure 6.8
Skimming

The name skimming comes from the process of skimming the cream from the top of a milk product (see figure 6.8).

Penetration pricing

Whilst skimming may be an appropriate policy when a seller is not sure of the elasticity of demand for the product, **penetration** pricing is appropriate when the seller knows that demand is likely to be elastic. A low price is therefore required to attract customers to the product. Penetration pricing is normally associated with the launch of a new product for which the market needs to be penetrated. Because price starts low, the product may initially make a loss until consumer awareness is increased. A typical example would be that of a new breakfast cereal. Initially it would be launched with a relatively low price, coupled with discounts and special offers. As the product rapidly penetrates the market, sales and profitability increase. Prices can then creep upwards. Penetration pricing is particularly appropriate for products where economies of scale can be employed to produce large volumes at low unit costs. Products which are produced on a large scale are initially burdened by high fixed costs for research, development and purchases of plant and equipment. It is important to quickly spread these fixed costs over a large volume of output. Penetration pricing is also common when there is a strong possibility of competition from rival products.

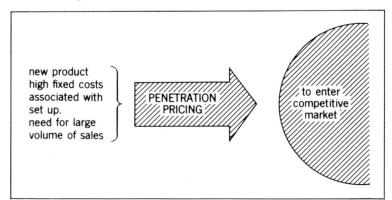

Figure 6.9
The environment in which penetration pricing may be appropriate

Destroyer pricing

A policy of **destroyer** pricing can be used to undermine the sales of rivals or to warn potential new rivals not to enter a particular market. Destroyer pricing involves reducing the price of an existing product or selling a new product at an artificially low price in order to destroy competitors' sales. This type of policy is based on long-term considerations and is likely to lead to short-term losses. The policy is most likely to be successful when the company that initiates it has lower costs than its competitors or potential rivals. However, it cannot be sustained in the long term because it will erode the profit base required to initiate research and development projects.

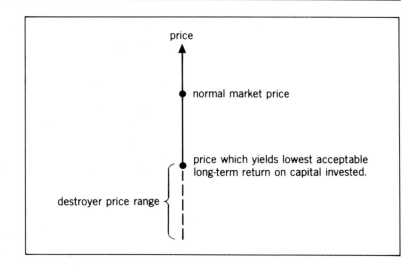

Figure 6.10
Destroyer pricing

Pricing and the marketing mix

In this chapter, we have concentrated on the importance of pricing decisions. However, pricing is used to complement other elements in the marketing mix. The marketing department will carefully consider how it can use price to complement place, promotion, and product.

Pricing decisions need to be accompanied by:

- product differentiation to produce the required benefits for customers.
- careful segmentation, so that benefits are promoted to those who appreciate them most.
- development of valid non-product features, such as better delivery, and after-sales service.
- improvement of product strengths.
- attention to company and product image.

CASE STUDY

A well-established chocolate firm is about to launch a new sweet bar on the market. The marketing manager thinks that about 100 million bars a year will be sold. The total cost of producing and advertising the new product will be £20 million a year.

Task 1

a Explain what is meant by direct and indirect costs.

b What direct and indirect costs might arise as a result of producing a new sweet bar?

Task 2

The firm hopes to make a 25% profit on each bar sold. At what price should the firm sell the sweet bar? Give your reasons.

Task 3

You are the firm's Advertising Manager. Write a brief report for the Board of Directors explaining which advertising media should be used for the new sweet bar.

Task 4

How might other sweet manufacturers react to the launch of the new sweet bar?

Task 5

How might the firm use any profits it makes from the new sweet bar?

Promotional pricing

Prices can be lowered from time to time to promote a product. **Promotional** pricing can be used to inject fresh life into an existing product or to create interest in a new product. Promotional pricing can be employed to increase the rate at which a product turns over. This can be used to reduce levels of stock or to increase the rate of activity of a business. A form of promotional pricing is the use of loss-leaders. Supermarkets frequently use loss-leaders to boost sales. A loss-leader is a good which is either marked down by the supermarket from its buying price or it is sold at no profit at all. Only a small number of the items sold by supermarkets are loss-leaders. The aim of selling them is to give the impression that all your items are cheap. A shopper seeing that cornflakes are 10p per packet cheaper in one supermarket may falsely expect all prices to be cheaper in that store.

CASE STUDY

Bottled water makes milk and petrol appear cheap

(*Adapted from The Independent, 16th February 1990.*)

People are paying up to a third more for mineral water that bubbles naturally out of the ground than they are for petrol, which has to undergo a complex drilling and refining process.

A litre of 4-star petrol now costs about 41p, and a litre of unleaded petrol about 39p. A bottle of Perrier water costs about 61p in a supermarket and up to 75p in a corner shop.

Aqua Libra, a mixture of spring water and juices costing more than £2 a litre, is five times as expensive as semi-skimmed milk, which costs 44p a litre in supermarkets.

Producing mineral water on a large scale – Perrier sold more than 200 million bottles in the United Kingdom last year – demands substantial investment in machinery. But once a plant is running, the process is comparatively cheap because the product itself costs virtually nothing.

At the Perrier spring at Vergèze in France, boreholes are sunk into the hillside. The water is channelled into the factory, and the gas that gives the drink its natural fizz is drawn off until the bottling takes place. A Perrier spokesman described it as a 'highly technical, highly automated operation.'

The water is bottled at source, packed into boxes and shipped to countries all over the world.

According to published trade estimates, 22% of what the consumer pays for a litre of mineral water goes on processing and distribution, 22% on the cost of the bottle, 16% on advertising, and 13% on VAT. The manufacturer takes 5% in profit and the retailer 22%.

The cost to the consumer of a litre of petrol – about 40p – breaks down very differently. A Shell UK spokesman said 62% went on VAT and duty, 6% to the retailer, and 32% to cover refining, distribution and marketing (including, in recent years, a Shell profit of about 1%).

The crude oil component in a litre of petrol accounts for about 16% of the cost, and this is divided between Shell and the retailer.

Crude oil is transported from oil wells to refineries around the world, and petrol is made by combining various products of the refining process. Petrol is shipped from refineries to national terminals, transferred to road tankers and delivered to filling stations.

Dairies pay more than 50% of the cost of a litre of milk in order to acquire the milk in a raw state. The Milk Marketing Board sells untreated milk to dairies for 23p a litre, and spends about 4% of the proceeds – 1p per litre – on marketing and administration, and on transporting the milk from the farms. The remainder is divided among the farmers who supplied the milk.

Task 1

Draw a chart to illustrate the respective breakdowns of costs and profits involved in producing milk, petrol and bottled water.

Task 2

How would you account for the differences in prices between the three products discussed in the article?

Task 3

What pricing policies would you recommend to a firm wishing to enter each of the three markets outlined. Explain your answer in depth.

Task 4

How important is price in the marketing mix of each of the products outlined? (For example, is price the most important single element? Explain in depth.)

CHAPTER

7

Distribution

Distribution is the process of moving goods and services to the places where they are wanted. It may involve a single step, or any number of steps. The local baker might supply bread directly to customers. In contrast, the furniture store may supply chairs and tables produced in Scandinavia which have passed through a number of hands and have been stored two or three times before arriving at their final destination. The transport network helps to bring the system of distribution together. Today, the communications links which are essential to effective distribution will frequently be co-ordinated by information technology, as we shall see later on in the chapter.

Transport

Transport costs can be a key cost component in many products. Choosing the 'best' possible transport system involves weighing up and 'trading off' a number of key components. What forms of transport should be used? (road, rail, air, sea etc) Can these forms of transport be integrated? What are the best possible routes? Do you use your own fleet or outside carriers? How do you maximise safety? How do you minimise costs? How do you make sure that products arrive on time and in the best possible condition?

Different forms of transport

Different forms of transport have their own distinctive advantages and disadvantages. Pipelines are expensive to construct, cheap to run, and expensive to repair. Roads give door-to-door delivery, are fast over short, and some long distances and make it possible to use your own fleet relatively cheaply. However, road travel is also subject to traffic delays, breakdowns, and drivers are limited to working only so many hours in a day. Rail transport is cheap and quick over long distances, particularly between major cities. However, it is not always appropriate for reaching out-of-the-way destinations and is costly for guaranteed speedy deliveries. Air is very fast between countries, providing the ultimate destination is not off the beaten track. Air is generally used for carrying important, urgent, relatively light and expensive loads. Sea transport is a cheap way of carrying high volume bulky loads.

Containerisation of loads has made possible the integration of these different forms of transport. Routes and services have been simplified to cut out wasteful duplication. Special types of vehicles have been designed to carry special loads. Direct motorway connections between major cities have proved to be of major importance in determining location decisions, coupled with fast intercity rail services, as well as air links. Different methods of transport may prove to be more or less cost effective in different situations depending on the cost of transport relative to the type of good being transported, the price of the good, or the speed with which it is needed. Heavy bulky items may be sent by road, rail or sea depending on the distances involved. Urgent items such as first-class post or important medical supplies may be sent by air.

CASE STUDY Reducing transport costs at Shell

Figure 7.1

Greater cost effectiveness is a worthwhile target. Over the past few years, Shell Transport has reduced the cost per tonne of product transported of oil by £2 – a 20% reduction.

This increased efficiency is based on a number of factors:

- the UK's improved road system
- larger more efficient road tankers
- non-rush-hour deliveries
- better driving techniques
- better planning systems (to translate hundreds of thousands of orders a year into sensible delivery schedules)
- better information systems (details of backlogs of orders to be delivered and other information, such as every order from the distribution terminals is now available on the PC of everyone who needs the information)
- more efficient handling of customer orders and payments
- investment in depots
- use of contracts
- use of salaried drivers
- maintenance of safety at all times
- working closely with refineries

Task 1
Which of the benefits outlined above are **a** internal econo-mies of scale (ie economies resulting from the expansion of

Shell itself, **b** external economies (ie economies resulting from growth outside of Shell).

Explain how these economies influence the unit cost of Shell petrol to the pumps? What are the implications for pricing?

Task 2
What are the costs of using larger delivery vehicles **a** to Shell **b** to groups and individuals external to Shell?

Task 3
What future developments can you foresee which will affect distribution costs of petrol? Explain what the effects will be.

Channel design decisions

Every business must continually re-appraise its existing channels. It must question the effectiveness of existing routes. From time to time they will need to be re-organised.

It is important to establish what your major objectives are. You will then need to explore any constraints in achieving these objectives and examine possible alternatives. These alternatives will then need to be evaluated before a decision can be made as to how to plan your channels.

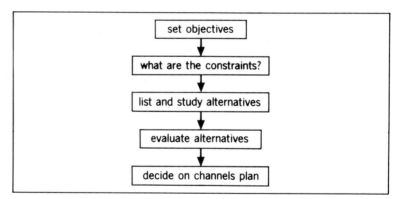

Figure 7.2
Planning channels

The channel is the route to your customer. In defining your objectives you will need to consider:

● the characteristics of your product. Is it bulky? Fragile? An urgent delivery? Heavy? Light?

● your customers' needs. Do they want it now? Do they want it packed? Do they want it labelled? Do they want door-to-door delivery?

● the nature of the competition. What are your rivals offering? Can you match them on delivery times and conditions?

● the nature of the middlemen involved. How efficient are they? Do they meet the standards expected by consumers?

These, and other factors, need to be considered in setting your objectives. For example, if your over-riding objective is to supply customers the day after a product has been manufactured for the lowest price on the market, you will need to discover the quickest and most effective channels with the least delays, you will also need to know how your rivals are operating and what they are offering.

When examining the alternative channels, you will need to map out different possibilities. If you want to reach a mass market you may want your product to be distributed through a wide number of channels. Alternatively, you may give exclusive rights to certain dealers or intermediaries. You will need to specify who does what at each stage of your alternative distribution maps. If a particular route looks as if it will cause problems and frictions it may need to be scrapped in favour of a smoother route.

Three main criteria will be used in evaluating channel alternatives. These criteria are:

1   economic

2   control

3   adaptive.

In evaluating the economic performance of alternative routes, you will need to weigh up costs against revenues in order to make profit calculations.

Control is also a major consideration. It is important to be able to have a fair measure of control over distribution. Your customers will blame you for breakdowns and problems. It is little help to blame an intermediary. The florist who won her first export order and sent her flowers by an external carrier that took ten days instead of three, lost the contract.

A distribution channel should also be able to be adapted to changing circumstances. If your route is inflexible then you may be storing up problems for the future.

When all of these factors are carefully weighed up, a channel plan can be put into effect. It will then need to be carefully monitored and evaluated. Ongoing considerations will include such factors as customer delivery time, the treatment of lost or damaged goods, cost of operation, the contribution of distribution to sales and many other factors.

Physical distribution

The physical distribution system balances the need for customer service against the need to minimise costs. To maximise customer service potential, you may need a lot of stock and warehousing space, considerable distribution staff, and rapid transport. However, to minimise costs you will need the reverse – minimum stock, limited storage space, skeleton staff and slow transport. Designing a physical distribution system therefore involves trading off costs against service, or inputs against outputs.

Inputs include all your distribution costs, that is freight costs + inventory costs + warehousing costs + other service costs. It is important to take a detailed account of these costs and to see how they can be controlled to minimise waste. It is important to be able to find out the distribution cost of every product you deal in. This involves a detailed analysis of how much labour time, transport time, and other factors are spent on each product.

Outputs can primarily be measured in terms of the value of services to customers. Distribution can give a clear competitive benefit in meeting customer needs, for example for a quick, prompt and efficient service. Every business must decide whether it is going to give a better, the same, or worse distribution service than its competitors. Weaknesses in distribution will clearly need to be compensated for by strengths in other areas of the marketing mix.

Alternative systems

The system that you come up with will depend largely on the scale of your operations and the size of the market you work in. If you operate from a single plant you may try to locate in a central market position, alternatively you may choose the spot with the best transport and communications links. (For example, a business handling a lot of international mail may choose to locate near Heathrow airport.)

A business operating a single plant with several markets, can choose whether to distribute directly from the plant or through a range of localised intermediaries.

A firm with several plants and several markets must weigh up a range of possible channels. Do you use the same distribution channels for all your products, or do you set up specialist routes? Clearly, in this situation distribution is a key business area.

Inventory control

A business that wants to maximise customer service will have the highest inventory costs, because it needs to hold stock to meet all foreseeable requests. The key inventory decisions are when to order and how much to order. The danger of keeping too little in stock is that you may lose custom because of dissatisfaction with the quality of your service. In contrast, too much stock adds to cost and wastage through goods becoming soiled.

Who is responsible for physical distribution?

Quite clearly distribution is a key area of marketing. It should be seen as a very important part of meeting customer needs and requirements. Responsibility for physical distribution is often shared between the Sales Manager, Inventory Control Manager, and Transport Manager – it is imperative however that these functions are centrally co-ordinated through marketing.

Industrial products (machines, bulldozers, expensive computer systems, etc.) are commonly sold by the maker directly to the user. Consumer goods (clothes, food, games, sports equipment etc) are more usually distributed through retail shops. The maker could supply the shops directly, but to do this the company would need a large salesforce. An alternative is to use wholesalers who buy in bulk and can be served by a small salesforce. The wholesaler is part of the chain of distribution and is a link between the manufacturer and the retailer, as shown in figure 7.3.

Manufacturer
(maker)
↓
Wholesaler
(storer)
↓
Retailer
(final seller)
↓
Customer
(buyer)

Figure 7.3
The traditional channel of
distribution

Channels of distribution

Choosing channels for distribution involves highly important policy decisions because distribution decisions can have an important effect on other areas of the marketing mix, such as price, promotion and product. For example, if you choose to distribute through a chain of readily accessible cut-price stores this will have the obvious implications for the public perception of your product. In addition, choosing a channel for distribution can be a long term commitment which can not be easily altered. For example, investing in your own transport fleet is an expensive outlay.

Considerations in preparing distribution channels
Who will be involved?

A number of important questions need to be addressed when establishing a new channel or modifying an existing one. Some of these are outlined below.

How many stages will be incorporated? Will the stages be internal or external to a company? (ie will it have its own transport fleet and storage facilities?) Will it involve direct marketing with no channel stages?

Many large companies today try to concentrate on their key production functions. This means that distribution is increasingly left to outside carriers working on a contract basis.

How tight will distribution be?

Some manufacturers require a very tight distribution schedule. Nowhere is this more true than in the distribution of fresh food. Deliveries need to arrive fresh in the stores in the early hours of the morning, the day after production. A tight delivery schedule will need to be planned over a 24-hour period with products meeting very precise deadlines. Similarly, in the distribution of petrol, sales need to be carefully monitored by computer-based capture of data at the pumps. Regular, scheduled deliveries need to be made to ensure steady stocks in the tanks. In other product areas more flexibility is required. Beer and ice cream distribution schedules need to vary considerably with the seasons. Other items require even more flexibility. For example, in the book trade, whilst bookshops can predict fairly accurately the sales of best-sellers they need to order many other types of books on a one-off basis, for individual customers. The distribution of newspapers fluctuates widely both on a seasonal basis, with trends in the market, and even on a day-to-day basis – for example when a sensational headline is produced.

How much training is required for distribution staff?

Modern distribution systems require skilled staff. This is particularly true with the advent of information technology systems and **just-in-time** philosophies. Nearly every member of staff in a large supermarket will need some form of training in data capture and data handling systems. Staff will need an understanding of the importance of quality and of meeting deadlines. Shell UK for example has its own fleet of 400 road tankers, each capable of carrying 34 000 litres of fuel. Safety is of paramount importance in supply and distribution operations. Safety concepts, training and skill enhancement are all part of an important programme for Shell tanker drivers. A modern computer system called AID (**Automated Integrated Distribution**) is a major element of the distribution operation, providing constant information. Another programme, **Oilstock**, keeps a constant track of product stocks and movements.

Types of channel flows

Distribution is not only about getting the product to the consumer. Several other flows are also involved. The title of ownership of the goods will need to go to the purchaser – this may be in the form of a receipt or invoice.

Payment will need to flow from the purchaser to the seller. Information will need to flow between the buyer and the seller. The seller needs to make clear what the terms of the offer are. The buyer needs to specify his or her requirements. The seller needs to promote the product to the buyer (see figure 7.4).

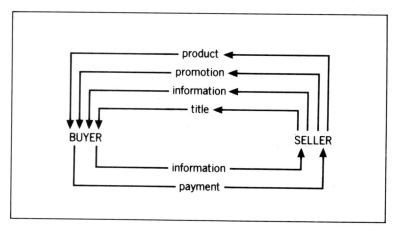

Figure 7.4
Types of channel flow

Nowadays, it is common practice for producers to try and integrate these flows. For example, the receipt is frequently complemented by promotional material, detailed information is given out with the product, etc.

CASE STUDY

Planning a delivery system

Planning a delivery system has to take into account many factors – geography, population, distribution, sales patterns, location of supply sources, road usage patterns (to avoid rush hours), available means of communication, competitive activities, availability of finance. All these factors are liable to change at short notice or with no notice!

Choosing a distribution network means taking a number of relevant factors into consideration and attempting to weigh them up in relation to each other. Sometimes, a ranking technique can be fed into a computer programme to give appropriate weights to relevant factors. Factors affecting distribution are assigned weights relative to their importance, and each channel is examined and ranked in terms of each factor. When ranks have been multiplied by the weighting factor and the scores totalled, the desirability of routes can be compared:

eg

factor	weight	alternative routes			
		A	B	C	D
supply location	7	1 / 7	2 / 14	3 / 21	4 / 28
geography	2	4 / 8	3 / 6	1 / 2	2 / 4
road usage patterns	4	1 / 4	4 / 16	2 / 8	3 / 12
competitive activities	2	1 / 2	2 / 4	3 / 6	4 / 8
population distribution	3	2 / 6	3 / 9	1 / 3	4 / 12
sales pattern	6	4 / 24	3 / 18	2 / 12	1 / 6
available communications	2	2 / 4	1 / 2	4 / 8	3 / 6
totals					

Figure 7.5
Using a ranking technique

In the example above, the rank attached to the relative importance of each factor for each location appears in the top left-hand corner of each cell and the rank multiplied by weight appears underneath the diagonal.

Task

a Which is the most desirable location?

b Feed the information provided by the chart into a spreadsheet.

  (i) What would be the most desirable route if the weighting of supply location was reduced from 7 to 1?

  (ii) If the ranking of locations in terms of geography was altered to A=1, B=2, C=3, D=4, and the ranking of sales pattern wass altered so that D became 2 whilst C became 1. If at the same time, the weight of competitive activities was raised to 3 and population distribution reduced to 2, what would be the outcome?

c Why might the supply location (i) have its weight reduced (ii) have its weight increased?

d Why is population distribution an important weighting factor?

e   Which of the factors listed influencing distribution routes are (i) largely within the control of an oil company (ii) largely beyond the control of an oil company?

f   In what circumstances is a computer programme a good way of planning distribution routes?

g   In what circumstances would computer programmes be ineffective for planning distribution routes?

Why use intermediaries in the process of distribution?

By contracting out the process of distribution a company can concentrate on its core functions. Manufacturers may lack the financial resources required to carry out their own expensive direct marketing operation. For example, the author of a book may be able to produce a very good end product. However, he or she will frequently lack the time, know-how, contacts, and money required to promote his or her book to all the potential book-stores that could carry their work.

In addition, the expense of direct marketing often requires that several complementary products are sold at the same time. A shop that simply sold talcum powder would be unlikely to succeed. A chemist's shop sells hundreds of different complementary products, made by several manufacturers.

The intermediary is a specialist. When you sell your products through a middle person you will benefit from their expertise in a wide range of areas – such as advice on packaging, pricing and where to sell.

The function of the wholesaler

Some people argue that intermediaries add to costs. The intermediary takes a cut from handling a product and thus increases price.

CASE STUDY

The price of a compact disc in January 1989

The figure below illustrates the breakdown of the price of a compact disc.

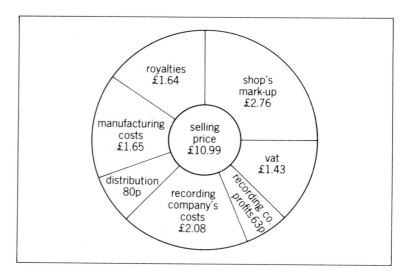

Figure 7.6

Task 1

What percentage of the price is taken up by the distribution and selling process? What arguments would you put forward to justify these distribution costs? Would the consumer benefit from the removal of the retailer from the chain? Explain your reasoning.

Advantages of the wholesaler

It is also possible to argue that the wholesaler provides many valuable functions, for example:

Breaking bulk

Manufacturers produce goods in bulk for sale but they do not want to store the goods themselves. They want to be paid as quickly as possible. A number of wholesalers buy the stock off them and generally payment is prompt. The wholesaler then stocks these goods – along with others bought from other manufacturers – on their premises, ready for purchase by retailers.

Simplifying the process of distribution

The chain of distribution without the wholesaler would look something like figure 7.7.

Manufacturer 1 has to carry out four journeys to supply Retailers 1, 2, 3, and 4. He or she has to send out four sets of business documents, and handle four sets of accounts. The same situation applies to each of the manufacturers so that in total, 16 journeys are made and 16 sets of paperwork are required. (This is a vast simplification – in the real world we may be talking about thousands of different transactions.)

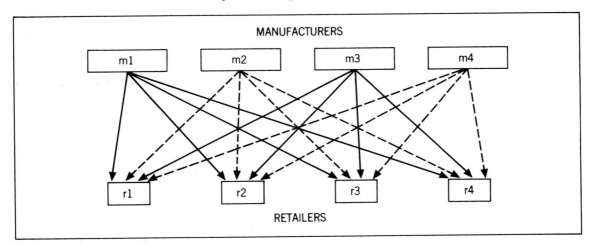

Figure 7.7   The wholesaler can simplify the costs and processes of distribution in the following ways:

● cutting down on transport journeys, fuel and other costs

● cutting down on paperwork, eg invoicing, administration and other costs.

The chain of distribution *with* the wholesaler would look something like figure 7.8 below. With the wholesaler everything is simplified.

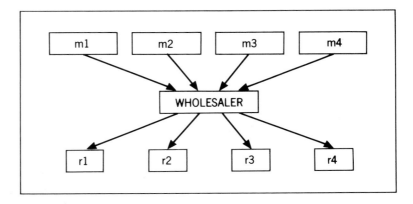

Figure 7.8

Storage

Most retailers only have a limited amount of storage space. The wholesaler can be looked upon as a huge storage cupboard for the retailer. Provided the retailer agrees to take supplies at regular intervals, the wholesaler will perform this important storage function. With the growth of cash-and-carry facilities, it has become easier for the retailer to stock up on supplies that are running down.

Packing and labelling

The wholesaler will sometimes finish off the packaging and labelling of goods, perhaps putting price tags on goods or brand labels for supermarkets.

Offering advice

Being in the middle of the process of distribution, wholesalers have a lot more information at their fingertips than either the retailer or the manufacturer. In particular, wholesalers know what goods are selling well. With this in mind they can advise retailers on what and what not to buy and manufacturers on what and what not to make.

Some wholesalers handle a wide range of general merchandise, but the majority specialise in particular lines (tobacco, steel etc). Many outlets are small and operate within a relatively small geographical area. In contrast, a number (particularly in the grocery trade) are large and have regional and even national distribution. The largest single unit in the wholesale trade is the **Co-operative Wholesale Society** (CWS). The CWS manufactures many lines of its own, owns interests overseas (eg tea estates in India), and owns its own shipping and transport fleet.

The last twenty years have seen the growth and development in the importance of cash-and-carry, and voluntary groups, in wholesaling.

Cash-and-carry

Most small retailers buy a large proportion of their stock from a **cash-and-carry**. The retailer is responsible for transporting his or her own goods from the wholesale warehouse to their premises. They are able to buy the goods at a discount.

The inside of a cash-and-carry is very similar to that of a large supermarket, except that goods are packed in bulk and the premises are sparsely decorated.

Voluntary groups

Some wholesalers have organised **voluntary groups** (see figure 7.9).

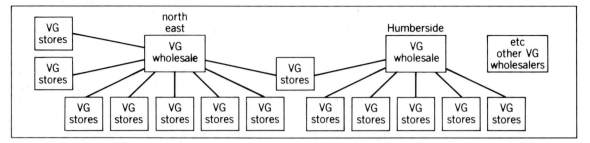

Figure 7.9
Voluntary groups

A voluntary group is an organisation set up by wholesalers and is made up largely of small retailers (the VG stores in figure 7.9) who have agreed to buy most of their stock from the group wholesaler. For example, the retailers might be bound by contract to purchase at least 70% of their supplies from group wholesalers. You will be able to identify some well known small shops operating under the voluntary group system from among names like, the Late Shop, Happy Shopper, VG, Spar, Mace, and Wavyline. The group wholesaler buys goods in bulk from manufacturers at discount prices and is able to pass these low prices onto the retailers. The Voluntary Group movement was a reaction to the growth in power and influence of chains of supermarkets that were undercutting the small corner shop from the mid-1960's onwards.

Retailing

The French word '*retailler*' means to cut again. We have already seen that the wholesaler breaks bulk supplies from the manufacturer. The retailer then cuts the bulk once again to sell individual items to consumers.

There are a number of categories associated with retailing which can be used in any classification system. These distinguishing features include:

Ownership

Who owns the retail unit? Is it independently owned by a sole trader? Is it owned by a large multiple with shareholders? Is it a co-operative? Is it a franchise outlet?

Range of merchandise

Does the retail outlet specialise in a narrow range of goods or does it have a spread of interests? Examples of specialist outlets would include an ice cream parlour, a furniture store, or a fast food outlet. A more general outlet would include a John Lewis Store, or Woolworths. Harrods at one time claimed to sell everthing from 'a pin to an elephant'. In some of the large French hypermarkets you can literally purchase a cement mixer within yards of the cheese counter.

Pricing policy

Some retail outlets concentrate at the bottom price range. They offer discounts and low prices. They buy in bulk and sell large quantities. The early policy of Jack Cohen, founder of Tesco, was 'pile them high – sell them cheap.'

In contrast, other retail outlets are characterised by an up-market price image. This is true of exclusive fashion shops, clothing and jewellery stores. Here, even if turnover is low, mark-up is several hundred per cent for many items.

In between these two extremes we will have mid-market pricing strategies as we have discussed in Chapter 6.

Location

Low price stores frequently choose locations where business rates and other site costs are minimised. In contrast, large multiples and department stores need a town centre location, or a situation near a major road. Small localised shops need a healthy volume of local custom for their livelihood — their strength resting in local convenience. They often alienate customers by having a high mark-up on goods.

Size

Many variety stores are now over 50 000 square feet, but superstores and hypermarkets have areas from 25 000 to 100 000 sq ft.

Types of retailers

Independent traders

The Census of Distribution classifies an independent trader as a retail organisation with fewer than ten branches. The average number is one or two. The market share and number of independent traders have been declining, particularly in food.

Many small shops in this country are owned by one person whose business interests are confined to a single shop. These small retailers often set up in business by putting their savings into starting up the shop. They then buy their stock by borrowing money from the bank and paying it back when they have sold their goods.

Advantages of the independent trader	Disadvantages of the independent trader
Personal relationship with customers. They are convenient for shoppers, providing a local 'round the corner' service. Can buy in stock to meet personal requirements of customers. Can work longer hours. Low overheads, low site costs. Benefits from joining voluntary group. Can offer personal credit facilities to shoppers. Can do home deliveries.	Price competition from multiples who are aided by buying economies and scale of operations. The owner needs to be a 'Jack of all trades' frequently lacking specialist retailing knowledge. Lack of capital to expand or improve business. Located away from high volume sales areas. Growth of use of cars has led to one-stop shopping in large shopping centres.

Figure 7.10
Advantages and disadvantages of the independent trader

The independent retailer has continued to decline throughout the last few decades of the twentieth century. Joining a voluntary group has proved to be the best route to survival for the independent shop owner. Niche marketing has also provided opportunities, for example the spread of independent stores selling 'vegetarian foods'.

Multiple chains

Multiple chains are organised as **joint stock companies**, with a high degree of control being exercised by professional managers. The definition given by the Census of Distribution is that a multiple store has more than ten branches. Some multiples are classified as specialist stores – concentrating on a narrow range of items such as clothing (eg Dorothy Perkins, Top Man and Austin Reed). Others are variety chains like Marks & Spencer and Boots. Others fall between these extreme definitions. WHSmith stocks records, stationery, magazines, newspapers and books as well as having its own travel agents on site.

Key features of a multiple organisation include:

- buying from the centre (in bulk at a discount).
- concentration of fast moving lines. They frequently sell products which are brand leaders or sell their own store labels.
- merchandise is widely known, often through national advertising.
- they tend to be located in 'busy' shopping areas, clustered together with other well-known multiples (usually High Street and shopping centre locations.)
- prices are usually relatively low. Volume sales are made.
- the shops project a strong corporate image. Easily recognised shop signs, distinctive colours and logos and uniform store fittings all project a unified image. (For example, Laura Ashley has its own central department for decorating and furnishing new stores and revamping existing ones. Stores have distinctive layouts, decor, and furnishings.)
- many key functions are centralised, for example accounting, advertising, recruitment, public relations, training and operating policies.
- most multiples are members of the **Multiple Shops Federation**. This is a combined pressure group and sounding-board for ideas from many of the well-known multiples.

Multiples are continuing to expand in importance. During the late 1980s, many new multiples developed in particular niches of the retailing market, in the wake of the success of the Body Shop. Other examples include Knickerbox and Tie Rack. With the downturn of the economy in 1989–90 these shops were hit particularly hard as consumer spending was checked. It remains to be seen whether this trend will continue to be reversed with changing economic fortunes.

Supermarkets and hypermarkets

A **supermarket** is defined as a store with at least 2000 square feet of selling area, using mostly self-service methods and having at least three check-out points. Supermarkets are a key feature of shopping in the 1990s. New and large supermarkets continue to be developed in most areas of population growth. Supermarkets have thrived with the development of brand names, the increasing number of working women with less time for shopping, and consumer preferences for easy shopping at low prices. Supermarkets benefit from low prices. They have high turnovers at a low mark-up. By maximising sales, they are able to spread their operation costs over a large output in order to minimise unit costs. The layout of a store is designed to speed customer flow and reduce time spent in shopping. In recent years, supermarkets have been able to meet consumer demands for green and organic products by using their considerable clout to influence producers. Because the supermarket business is highly competitive, it is also responsive to consumer preference changes.

Hypermarkets are large supermarkets. They have a massive selling area and offer a very wide range of household goods at discount prices. As well as food and clothing, they stock lines as diverse as DIY equipment, motoring accessories, cosmetics, children's toys and hardware. They aim to provide cheaply for all the basic shopping needs of an average household. They may also contain restaurant facilities and stock consumer durables like television sets at a discount. They are usually located on the outskirts of towns where building land is cheaper.

They use all the latest technology to full advantage. Computerised till service feeds directly into a central computer which prints out an itemised bill for the customer. At the same time, the information about what goods have been sold is fed into the computer; the ordering department is continually aware of how goods are moving and which need re-ordering, so that there should never be any shortages.

Department stores

The definition of a **department store**, as used by the Census of Distribution, is a store with a large number of departments employing more than twenty-five people. Department stores are to be found on 'prime sites' in high streets in most towns and cities. A department store:

- is divided into separate departments, each with a departmental manager and staff.
- provides a very wide range of services so that customers can do all their shopping under one roof.
- provides a high standard of service and comfort with carpeted floors, pictures on the walls, restaurant and café services, art galleries, exhibitions and displays, as well as polite service to customers.
- often charges slightly higher prices for quality goods (it also charges higher prices to cover its high overheads such as high rates in the city centre). However, whilst it is true that department stores tend to have an up-market image, they can also use their advantages, created by bulk buying and large scale, to offer discount prices on many items. For example, the John Lewis group have the trading motto: 'Never knowingly undersold'.

Department stores continue to be a force in the market place with their reputation for quality and service and the added incentive of credit accounts. In the last decade they have moved increasingly to customer self-selection. They have also operated a policy of 'leasing' shopping space to other retail names with a compatible image. This makes better use of space and is an added attraction to consumers.

Discount stores

Today, specialist firms like Argos and Comet concentrate on selling large quantities of consumer durables at **discount** prices. The aim of these stores is to produce a high level of total profit by means of a very high rate of turnover of stock. As the name implies, they attract custom by the discounts they offer. In recent years, these stores have moved away from the original warehouse-like service, and have increasingly begun to offer credit services.

Discount stores tend to be located on edge of town locations. They are well-stocked with a wide range of models. Recent examples which will become very significant in the 1990s are discount toy sellers and discount pet food sellers. These are located in large centres of population where demand is constant and high.

Co-operative retail societies

Today there are fewer than thirty **co-operative retail societies** operating in various parts of the United Kingdom. There used to be several hundred, but over the years, many of the smaller societies have joined together. The largest one is called the **CRS** (which in the 1990s is likely to merge its operations with the Co-operative Wholesale Society.)

The Co-ops have always tried to do more than just run a shopping business. They set out to serve the local community in a variety of ways. For example, a Co-op will often support a local education service for members, subsidise health care and other social activities, as well as financing co-operative theatre ventures and recreational facilities.

To understand the basis of co-operation, it is helpful to look back to the origins of co-ops. The first retail co-operative was set up in 1844 by a group of twenty-eight weavers in Rochdale, Lancashire. They were fed up with being paid low wages in tokens which they could only exchange in company-owned shops, where prices were high. They clubbed together to buy foodstuffs from a wholesaler which were then sold to members. Profits were shared out amongst members in the form of a dividend, according to how much each had spent in the shop.

To become a shareholder in a modern co-operative retail society you need only buy a £1 share. Shareholders are entitled to attend meetings, to have a say in policy-making, and to elect the officers of the local society.

For many years the Co-ops tended to share out their profits by giving a dividend to members, often by issuing stamps to shoppers with every purchase. These stamps were stuck in books and could be traded in for cash or used to make further purchases. Today, only a few societies issue stamps. Instead, the Co-ops tend to plough their profits back into improving their stores. The CRS, for example, has opened up a number of 'Leo' hypermarkets in various parts of the country.

The Co-ops are preparing for the 21st century by making their stores bright and attractive and by selling a very wide selection of goods. Although they have closed down many small shops the twin aims of the co-op are still to provide profits and to serve the local community.

Mail-order firms

Mail-order firms sell goods either through agents or through members of the public ordering through a free catalogue. A mail-order agent will receive a commission of about 10% of the sales made. Some firms have their own delivery service, whilst others use the Post Office, or other carriers. Many goods sold by mail-order are paid for by credit.

Mail-order goods give good value for money because by cutting out the middleman, firms can sell goods at competitive prices. Mail-order firms are able to use computerised methods for handling orders and stocks and sell from large warehouses situated in locations where rates are cheap and communication links efficient.

Mail-order firms can be situated anywhere providing there are good transport links. They offer money back guarantees on items.

Franchising

In America, one-third of all retail sales are made through firms operating under the **franchise system**. It is a method of selling that is becoming increasingly popular in Britain.

A franchise is permission to market a product in a specified area. The person taking out the franchise puts up a sum of money as capital and is issued with equipment by the franchise company to sell or manufacture the product in which the franchise company deals. The firm that sells a franchise is called a **franchiser** and a person taking out a franchise is called a **franchisee**. The person taking out a franchise has the sole right of operating in a particular area. Franchising is common in 'fast-foods', examples being McDonalds and Spud-U-Like, and in the plumbing business, with Dyno-Rod.

Advantages to the franchisee	Advantages to the franchiser
Trades under a well known name eg Pizza Hut, Thorntons Has a local monopoly Works for him or herself, and receives most of the profits Is supplied with equipment and conception Receives training	Franchiser does not risk own capital Supplies equipment and training courses – which are tax deductible Takes a percentage of profits Has people working indirectly for them who will work long hours because they are also working for themselves.

Figure 7.11
Advantages of the franchising system

Direct selling

The most commonly quoted examples of **direct selling** are mail-order and direct response advertising, but these more often than not involve some form of intermediary. Mail-order firms usually buy the commodities that they sell through their catalogues in bulk from manufacturers. Direct response advertisers – such as firms that advertise in newspapers, leaflets delivered through letter boxes and in television advertisements giving the address of the firm – are often wholesalers who buy in bulk from manufacturers. It is therefore probably more accurate to say that direct selling means simplifying the chain of distribution to miss out the retailer.

Manufacturers can themselves cut out middlemen by owning their own retail units. Examples of this are breweries which own their own public houses, oil companies with their own petrol stations and textile manufacturers with their own 'factory shops'.

Television selling is already big business in the United States, Australia and other countries. In the United States, the Homes Shopping Network is a 24-hour viewing business, which became a huge success story in the late 1980s. Between 1986 and 1990 it grew into a $4 billion a year sales group.

The typical format is for each product to have a four-minute slot, during which time viewers can phone through on one of 200 freephone lines, order something and pay by quoting their credit card number. The products sold are mainly brand names presented in an entertaining and informative way.

Other forms of retailing

There are other forms of retailing, accounting for small segments of sales. These include door-to-door selling, mobile shops, street trading, automatic vending, and kiosks.

CASE STUDY

Consumers' crown shattered

The notion that the 'consumer is king' has become redundant, with shops all looking the same and offering a uniform range of goods at similar prices, market research chiefs claimed in a survey in June 1990.

Mintel argue that as we move towards the year 2000, customer service will be the key to retailing success.

Consumers are moving away from price and convenience to the service they receive in the store. To succeed, shops will have to train staff to be better informed about the products they sell.

Shops will need to take more account of local and regional consumer differences, and multiples might need to consider opening smaller neighbourhood outlets selling, for example, solely own-label convenience foods.

Price, quality and range will still be important features but better product information will be expected by consumers, especially the older 'sophisticated consumer'.

The report concentrates on three retail sectors – large electrical items, furniture and weekly grocery shopping. In a survey of about 1400 adults, 'helpful staff' was the most wanted improvement in electrical and furniture sectors. In furniture, more convenient delivery, for example outside normal working hours, and immediate availability, were also demanded (see figure 7.12).

LARGE ELECTRICAL ITEM		FURNITURE		WEEKLY GROCERIES		

Reason for store choice

LARGE ELECTRICAL ITEM	%	FURNITURE	%	WEEKLY GROCERIES	%	
Lowest prices	36	Competitive price	38	Convenience	42	
Previously bought from a store	25	Wide range	32	Car Parking	35	
Stock brand wanted	23	Browsing	29	Low prices	31	
Helpful staff	20	Quality of products	25	Well laid out store	30	
Wide range	19	Helpful staff	22			
		Services	21			

Improvements wanted

LARGE ELECTRICAL ITEM	%	FURNITURE	%	WEEKLY GROCERIES	All %	Housewives Only %
Helpful staff	59	Helpful staff	47			
Testing facilities	40	Convenient delivery	42			
Convenient delivery	32	Immediate availability	41	Faster checkout	47	48
Brochures/leaflets	27	After sales service	41	Shorter queues	42	46
Clearer pricing	22	More information	29	Better facilities	26	31
Better stock levels	20	Clearer pricing	20	Packers	24	33

Figure 7.12
Shoppers' attitudes when buying

Task 1

What do the results of the survey tell you about consumer choice when shopping for large electrical items, furniture and weekly shopping? What do you think will be the likely impact on the fortunes of the different types of retailers that have been outlined in this chapter?

Task 2

What do the results of the survey tell you about improvements sought by consumers in retail outlets selling large electrical items, furniture and weekly groceries? What changes are required in each of the retail outlets mentioned in this chapter to deal with these requirements? Are some retail types better placed than others to meet these requirements?

Task 3

How do you foresee the future of retailing developing? Which retail outlets will **a** thrive **b** stand still **c** decline. Explain your reasoning.

CASE STUDY   Morrisons wraps up bread distribution

In August 1990, WM Morrison supermarkets, the Bradford retailing group was able to report an increase of almost 30% in its bread business as a result of price cuts which left its own label 800g white and brown long-sliced loaves at 37p, as much as 10p below what was previously charged.

Behind the success in bread lies the centralised distribution from Wakefield where the group employed 500 people on a site which also included a grocery distribution centre and a fresh food centre.

Central distribution helped Morrisons to achieve an increase of about 20% in sales in money terms (15% in volume). But it was the success of the centralised bread distribution that caused the biggest sensation in the grocery trade, which handles 60% of bread sales.

The company made a study of the bread business in 1988. This showed that bread was costing more to sell and deliver than it was to make. That led to the decision to set up a central base at Wakefield.

Morrisons have taken over total company control of bread distribution to their supermarkets ranging from Carlisle to Newcastle in the North and Stamford to Telford in the South. They have been able to take a 'company view' on pricing and pass on the saving in distribution costs to the customer, rather than taking a 'supplier view'.

Morrisons' success owes much to the ability which centralised distribution has given them to exploit the fact that baking is a business with a high 80 to 90% breakeven point. In such conditions, volume orders become very important. Now Morrisons buy in very large quantities from bakers to their central warehouses, bakers are pleased to meet these contracts because they can produce in bulk, and keep down transport costs through sending full lorryloads to a single location.

Task 1

What is the difference between sales in money terms and sales volume? How important are these two indicators in assessing the performance of a business? What has been the key to Morrison's success in cutting bread prices? Are there lessons to be learnt for other business organisations?

Task 2

What is meant by the statement that 'they have been able to take a "company view" on pricing and pass on the saving in distribution costs to the customer rather than taking a "supplier view".' Why is this particularly important to a market-led company?

The role of automatic identification in retailing developments

Automatic identification is one of the fastest growing, but least known, sectors of the high technology industry.

It enables users to collect identifying information about large numbers of items without manual key-strokes and to feed the data into a computer.

The **auto ID sector**, as it is commonly called, originated in the early 1970s with the advent of bar coding on a small scale in the retailing, wholesaling and distribution industries. It took off in the late 1970s and early 1980s when supermarkets invested heavily in check-out scanners.

The essential parts of an auto ID system are a means of encoding the identifying information and applying it to the item in question, a machine to read the code and software to feed the encoded data into a computer for analysis.

Bar codes, familiar through their use of grocery packaging, account for about 70% of auto ID. The scanner passes a small laser beam across the printed code and detects the distribution of bars and spaces. A computer then converts this pattern into a number for processing.

The bar codes which are used today are entirely numeric. The system used for retailing in Europe, the European Article Number (EAN) gives each item a number – of up to 13 digits.

The suppliers of retail goods increasingly include a bar code on the outside of each item or its packaging. This is universal practice in the supermarket and grocery sector and is becoming so in book and magazine publishing.

Increasingly, bar code printers are combined with automatic labelling machines, or even with laminators to produce self-adhesive labels encapsulated in a clear protective coating.

Bar code readers are steadily becoming smaller, lighter, more powerful and more durable. A new generation of portable scanners, linked to powerful hand-held computers, is extending auto ID to new applications.

At the same time, **fixed scanners** are being developed to read labels at greater distances and faster speeds – up to 400 scans per second while making fewer than one error in a million scans.

Optical character recognition (OCR) another widely-used auto ID technique, also depends on printed symbols. Here the scanner converts letters and numbers into computer code. An obvious advantage of OCR is that the symbols can also be read by human beings, while a bar code only makes sense to a machine reader.

The most familiar non-optical technique for auto ID is the **magnetic stripe** applied to credit cards and other plastic cards used for personal identification and financial transactions. A magnetic stripe can store more information than a bar code and can easily be rewritten with new data, but it cannot be read at a distance and cannot be printed on cheaply. Most large retailing and wholesaling premises today have specialised departments which quickly deal with credit card and cheque transactions. This means that customers do not cause hold-ups at check-out points.

Far larger amounts of data can be stored on **smart cards** with embedded computer chips. However, as yet, these have little value in retailing.

For automatic identification at greater distances or in harsher environments than bar codes can cope with, **radio frequency** (RF) tags come into their own. These tags, which may be as small as a grain of rice, are embedded within the product – if necessary beneath a layer of protective material.

They contain a transponder, a tiny receiver/transmitter which sends out identifying data when it is activated by the system's interrogating antenna. RF tags can be read at a distance of up to one metre from the antenna and do not need a direct line of site. RF is used for identifying moving vehicles to speed up traffic flow at high security installations and car parks. Automatic road tolls are another application which allows tagged vehicles to pass without stopping to pay. The toll is electronically collected from drivers' accounts.

CHAPTER

8 Promotion

The process of communication

Since early days, individuals have used hand signals, vocal patterns, symbolic drawings and facial expressions for the purpose of communicating some form of message to one another. Today, the exchange of information takes place through sophisticated media such as interconnecting computers, fax machines, telephones and an endless variety of other methods, in order to accomplish the same goal. An efficient network of communications is essential for successful promotional activity. It enables an organisation not only to communicate with its customers but also to build up an image with the world at large. Such an image will help others to form a judgement about what the organisation stands for and will influence their dealings with it.

For marketing purposes, communication of products and services contributes to the persuasion process to encourage consumers to avail themselves of whatever is on offer. As all promotional activities involve an element of communication, an understanding of communication theory helps an organisation to make the most of its investment.

The process of communication involves sending **messages** to consumers through various channels or media in order to create **awareness** and **understanding** of why they might wish to buy particular products or services.

Organisations are the **senders** in the communication process and consumers are the **receivers**. A sender will put information in a form that a receiver can understand. This might involve using oral, visual, verbal or written messages to transmit the ideas. This process is called **encoding**. The sender will also choose a particular medium to use to send the message to the receiver, eg television, radio, newspapers etc. The consumer interprets the message through a process of **decoding**. If the consumer interprets the message as required, it should have the impact that the seller wished for.

Though the message flows through to the receiver there is no guarantee that the receiver will either receive the full message or even understand it. This is because the process may be subject to some form of interference which affects the flow of information. This is known as **noise** and may lead to the downfall of the message. It will take the form of any barrier which acts as an impediment to the smooth flow of information. It may include linguistic and cultural differences between the sender the receiver. Noise in the competing environment may affect communication so that the meaning of the message is lost. For example, adverts have to compete with other adverts. One leaflet may be lost in amongst the sea of direct mail we receive through our letterbox.

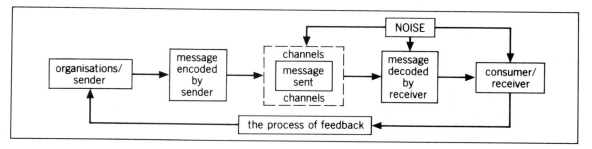

Figure 8.1
Communications process

To improve the chances of the message getting through, it may be necessary to repeat the message several times rather than relying upon one transmission. It might also be necessary to use a variety of channels of communication/media to avoid any noise in one particular channel.

Feedback from the receiver to the sender enables an organisation to monitor its performance and satisfy itself that the messages are getting through and are having the desired effect.

CASE STUDY   Video recorders

An advertiser's biggest enemy is rapidly becoming the video recorder. Though many are happy to sit through commercials during an evening's television, if they have taped their favourite programmes, they do not sit and admire the adverts but instead, fast-forward through the break.

In the US they call this the 'zapping' culture. A recent UK survey confirmed the worst fears of advertisers. Whereas 43% of viewers will sit through and watch live advertisements, if they are watching a pre-recorded programme, only 10% will watch them. Handsets add to the problem, and when in possession of a remote control, even more viewers whiz through the advertisements. One organisation – Rowntree Mackintosh – has been looking at how to adapt commercials for such a fast-forward operation. It claims to have looked into techniques where commercials could still be seen when being fast-forwarded so that the message could still get through.

Task 1
Describe how a remote control video recorder may lead to the downfall of a message.

Task 2
Analyse the elements of noise in your own household which affect your receiving advertising messages. How could advertisers – if at all – overcome such instances of noise?

Effective communications

A number of factors will determine the effectiveness of the process of communication. Personal factors such as linguistic, cultural and educational differences are bound to cause problems of encoding and decoding messages. Advertisers and their copywriters have to develop messages and express ideas so that their target market can understand them. Group factors or influences may also affect a message. Feelings about a particular product such as a motor car and its quality may be reinforced by group opinions. Message factors will also determine effective communication. The strength, clarity, duration and frequency of the message will be important as well as the type of media channel chosen.

Task

Make a list of ten advertisements that you have regularly come across. Construct a table similar to the one illustrated and comment briefly upon each advert in terms of personal, group and message factors. Also make a brief comment upon overall effectiveness. Compare your results with others and consider generally the important factors in an effective process of communications.

Advertisements	Personal Factors	Group Factors	Message Factors	Overall Effectiveness
1				
2				
3				
4				
etc				

Figure 8.2
Advertising effectiveness

The promotional mix

The promotional mix comprises all of the marketing and promotional communication methods used to achieve the promotional objectives of the marketing mix. These methods can be broken down into two distinct areas.

Non-controllable methods are marketing messages which take place on the basis of word-of-mouth, personal recommendations and a consumer's overall perception of a particular product or service. For example, consumer opinions are influenced by a number of factors, such as whether their family has regularly used the product. A brand heritage, character, colour and image will also have helped to create brand loyalty and influenced regular purchasing patterns. Perhaps the most famous brand heritage is that of Rolls Royce. The term 'a Rolls Royce' company is frequently applied to organisations which build up a strong reputation for their goods and services. On the other hand, public displeasure with a particular organisation may influence purchases, for example CFC's in aerosols and South African goods.

Controllable methods are marketing messages which are carefully directed to achieve the objectives of an organisation's promotional campaign. They include four main areas:

a   *Advertisements* are messages sent via the media which are intended to inform or influence the people who receive them.

b   *Sales promotions* are techniques designed to increase sales such as money-off coupons, free samples and competitions.

c   *Personal selling* involves the making of sales and emphasizes the importance of salesmanship.

d   *Publicity* is non-personal communication using the media but unlike advertising it is not quantified with the success of a particular product. It's key component is 'Public Relations'.

Some of these methods are discussed further in Chapter 9.

The controllable methods of promotion are often categorised as **above-the-line** or **below-the-line**. While changes in the law have since extinguished the origins of this system, the terms are still often used. Above-the-line refers to the media such as TV, radio and press, for which commission is paid to an advertising agency. Below-the-line media comprises all media and promotional techniques for which no commissions are paid to an agency, such as exhibitions, sales literature and direct mail.

Using the promotional mix

An organisation needs to appraise carefully the communications process. It must have a clear idea of what a message should be, to whom it should be sent and the expected outcome of sending it. Promotional requirements will vary with geographic size, demographic dispersion and market segmentation. The more clearly an organisation can define its particular market segment, the more relevant will be its promotional mix.

An organisation has to decide upon how to achieve its objectives. To do so it must formulate a strategy to use an appropriate blend of promotional techniques. A common mnemonic used to describe how to persuade a customer to make a purchase decision is A.I.D.A.:

A – a customer's *attention* is captured and they are made *aware* of the product.

I – an *impact* stimulates their *interest*.

D – they are persuaded that they are *deprived* because they do not have the product, and this helps to stimulate a *desire* or demand for it.

A – *action* involves the actual purchase of a product.

The most common method of setting a budget for promotional activities involves allocating a fixed percentage of sales revenue to promotion. Some producers of consumables have as much as 10% of their sales revenue devoted to promotion. It is always difficult to assess the effectiveness of promotional expenditure because the results may be delayed. A distinction is sometimes made between immediate-impact and delayed-impact advertising.

Whereas companies in consumer goods markets may commit anything up to 80% of their promotional budget on advertising and sales promotion to generate 'demand pull', where distributors stock the product because advertisers maintain demand, companies in organisational markets are likely to rely more upon personal selling and other forms of publicity. For example, in such markets catalogues and technical information may need to be supported by demonstrations, trials and testimonies from satisfied customers.

The promotional mix used must match the stages in the Product Life Cycle (see Chapter 4). For example, during the introduction stage, consumer awareness must be developed. As the product reaches maturity, it might be necessary to emphasize a brand's heritage to maintain consumer loyalty. Organisations must also react to the promotional expenditure of their competitors. For example if a brand of confectionery is advertised heavily, the sales of other brands might be affected unless the other manufacturers retaliate. In fact matching the activities of competitors is often a criterion for promotion, particularly to retain market share during the maturity phase.

CASE STUDY

The promotional budget

Manufacturers and retailers of consumer goods spend a large part of their promotional budget on advertising: brewers spend a large proportion of theirs on sales promotions, while banks spend nearly as much on brochures as they do on advertisements. These are just a few findings in a survey of the chief executives in advertising companies.

The survey showed that the promotional mix varied widely between industry sectors, with the computer industry spending the smallest proportion of their budget on advertising but the largest on exhibitions and training.

On average, across all industrial sectors, advertising took the biggest single slice out of the promotional budget followed by sales promotion.

Task 1
Explain why manufacturers of consumer goods will tend to spend more on advertising than a manufacturer of computers.

Task 2
Think carefully of an organisation whose product or service you use. From your position as a consumer, how do they seem to spend their promotional budget? Refer to any advertising, sales promotions, personal selling and publicity you have come across.

The business of advertising

As we saw earlier, advertisements are messages sent through the media which are intended to inform or influence the people who receive them. Such a message is paid for by an advertiser in order to sell a product or service or to seek support or participation. It includes adverts on TV, radio, and in magazines, but does not include promotional materials supplied with a product, promotional events, branding or company brochures. To assess how well promotional money is spent **DAGMAR** has today become a fundamental part of good advertising practice. This stands for:

Defining Advertising Goals For Measured Advertising Results.

Advertising agencies

To plan a campaign, an advertiser will consult an advertising agency. Such an agency is a vital link between the advertiser and the consumer. The rôle of an advertising agency is to create, develop, plan and implement an advertising campaign for their clients. The extent to which an agency does so will vary according to its type. Some agencies offer all kinds of services, others only buy media and others specialise in creative work. Such agencies offer skilled expertise which can be shared with clients. It would not be economic for the majority of advertisers to employ a full-time team. Agencies also offer the media an economic way of buying and selling airtime and space. The media will only have to deal with a small number of agencies compared to thousands of individual advertisers.

The team of experts in an advertising agency service clients who are known as **accounts**. An **account executive** will supervise work for a particular client and, together with the account director, will work to meet the client's objectives. To do this they will lead an account group comprising representatives from each of the main departments contributing to the compaign.

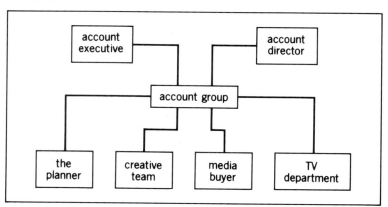

Figure 8.3
Composition of account group

The account executive has to understand the needs of the clients, their operations and their industry, and interpret those to the agency. They also have to present the agency's proposals to the client. The job requires diplomacy in order to keep all of the interested parties happy. **The planner** will assist the account executive, maintain the performance and timetable of activities and use specialist market research to assess the reactions of the public. From such analysis they can decide upon a strategy for a campaign and also test ads to see how the public respond. The **creative team** consists of an art director who will create and develop rough drawings or illustrations called **visuals** and a copy writer who produces the words known as **copy** for an advertisement. They will also commission further artwork for the ads. **The media buyer** buys 'space' or 'time' on TV, radio, newspapers and magazines. They will work with a media planner to decide the type of media to carry particular advertisements. The **TV department** will, where necessary, commission the production of a commercial, organise the shoot, and edit and supply the finished ad.

When taking on an account, an advertising agency will find out what sort of message the advertiser wants to give to the market. This will initially involve finding out as many facts as possible about the product, for example, its market segment, how it is sold, what its market share is and how its price compares with alternatives. The agency will not only wish to know about the product but also about the alternatives. To discover more, market research is used on a sample of consumers and the feedback is analysed.

At this stage, the agency starts to put forward some ideas for an advertising campaign. These are discussed with the client. The agency then provides ideas in the form of storyboards which will show roughly what the commercials/advertisements will look like. The roughs will be tested on the target audience and the campaign will then be carefully planned. The client will need to approve the ideas. Production then begins upon the final advertisement. A production company will be signed up to make the TV commercial and the media department will book suitable slots in television time as well as space in newspapers and magazines. A test launch may be used to test consumer reaction to the campaign. The campaign will then go national. Researchers will then follow up the campaign by finding out how the public responds to the ads and this will be fed back to the client so that they are aware of consumer reaction.

Agencies have in the past been paid by commission. The agency would book time or space for an advertiser who would then be charged by the media, who would pay a commission to the agency. The commission was paid by the media and not by the client. However, over recent years agencies have become more involved in below-the-line promotional activities and have therefore billed their clients for activities. Many agencies today charge a straight fee for their services and then reimburse any commissions from the media to their client.

CASE STUDY   The round tea bag

Lyons Tetley preyed on consumers' perceived need for comfort and reassurance with the round tea bag. The product initially relied upon the emotional satisfaction that tea drinkers glean from their habit. Tea is an established part of British culture – warm, sociable and comforting. Research showed that consumers preferred tea in a cup with a round bag. Though it tastes the same and contains exactly the same tea as the square counterpart, it looks better and fits more neatly into a cup.

Tetley's advertising agency D'Arcy, Masius, Benton and Bowles devised a campaign which retained brand loyalty by using the well established characters of the Tetley teafolk in a £3 million advertising spend. The television campaign centered upon the Beach Boys' song 'I Get Around'.

Task 1

Comment upon

a the round tea bag and the reasons for its introduction.

b the advert combining the Tetley teafolk and the Beach Boys' hit. Mention visual success, artistic merit, creativity and appeal to brand loyalty.

Task 2

How do you feel consumers have responded to such a campaign?

Task 3

Work in small groups to think of a product in a market that would be responsive to a minor product change to improve its appeal to consumers. Describe the changes you would make. Then:

a outline the target market for whom the new version of the product would be directed. Mention the particular market segment.

b plan a campaign. Consider what sort of promotional techniques you would use and the message you would try to transmit. Invent a **strapline** – a saying to be associated with the product. Produce a rough drawing, as well as some copy, and put them on a storyboard.

c choose the media you would use to promote the product.

d present the campaign suggestions to the rest of the group and assess their response to your ideas.

Creativity

The interaction of ideas together with creativity are a major factor in the success of an advertising campaign. The message might be a combination of words, symbols, characters, colours, sounds and gimmicks. It must be conveyed to the right people in the right place at the right time, as 'good' advertising will not work if it is misdirected.

It is always an important objective of an advertising campaign to develop a good rapport with the target consumer. Sometimes this is found out by discovering where interests lie and how they respond to different sorts of advertising strategies.

At the heart of creative advertising is good copywriting. Copy creates the theme for an advertising campaign and the visualiser/art director will develop ideas from the basic copy. Buzz words such as 'new', 'free' and 'call' are all designed to encourage the consumer to do something. They are action words. Straplines associated with a brand name can help to create an image. For example, 'Once driven, forever smitten' or 'Ralgex has the muscle'.

Some organisations use a character to identify with a brand, so that the actions of the character will help to protect the qualities of the product or service. These characters have often become valuable promotional assets. For example, Mr Kipling creates a home-baked image for cakes, Mr Sheen helps to reflect the qualities of furniture polish and we have already mentioned the Tetley teafolk.

Figure 8.4
Creating a home-baked image for cakes (*source: Manor Bakeries Ltd, a company within the Rank Hovis MacDougall plc group*)

A brand's heritage is often an area that advertisers like to build upon. It helps an organisation to foster brand loyalty – grandparents and parents often pass on their consumption habits to successive generations. For example, many confectionery products, such as Smarties, have been with us for more than fifty years.

Advertisements are enhanced by artwork – often the prime means of capturing the imagination of the consumer. Most mass media today have colour facilities; the newspapers are the most recent addition to the fold. Good artwork and effective use of colour can help to develop a unique brand or organisational identity which is instantly recognisable as a message as to the quality, reliability and acceptability of a product. Improvements in technology have provided artists with further opportunities to develop their work.

Humour is another area which is open to creative brilliance. For example, in the tea sector, fierce competition for awareness through humour takes place between Brooke Bond Oxo's chimps and the Tetley teafolk.

One of the secrets of successful advertising is repetition. Brand or company names can appear throughout an advertisement and be regularly repeated. It is also possible to create a sense of motion with a cleverly concocted strapline or invent a combination of words in a catchy style that consumers will probably always remember – such as 'we all adore a Kia-ora'.

Advertising messages help organisations to develop and communicate the identity of their brands as well as to provide a foundation for the other areas of the promotional mix.

CASE STUDY   ## Snappy lager slogans

One of the most interesting advertising areas over recent years has been the remarkably effective 'one-liner' lager advertising strategies. The grandaddy of them all is Heineken with its famous line 'Refreshes the parts other beers cannot reach'. Carling Black Label have also been effective with their 'I bet he drinks . . .' as has 'I wouldn't give a Castlemaine XXXX' and 'Malcolm the Mountie always gets his can.'

Many feel that the slogans have been successful because they adopt the language of the pub. Pub-goers swap jokes from the ads, discuss them and a sense of comradeship is created. This theory was recently borne out by market research investigating the effect of slogans on men and women. Recall of the slogans was much higher amongst men.

It has been said, however, that lager 'one-liners' are on the wane. An advertising agency recently withdrew its use of the 'It ain't heavy' slogan for Miller Lite. They feel that in the 1990s customers are becoming more sophisticated in their approach to advertising and expect more than just slogans. This new movement suggests that the days of the slogan are numbered and that instead we will see greater creativity surrounding the promotion of lager.

Task 1

Explain why you feel that lager slogans have been so successful.

Make a list of slogans that you can remember that refer to other products; comment briefly on what they are trying to achieve and their overall effectiveness.

Task 2

● If lager 'one-liners' are on the wane, what ought to replace them?

● Make a suggestion for a more thorough approach for a lager advertisement and discuss your ideas.

The Media

The characteristics of various media will recommend them to creative areas such as sound, vision and script. The success of an advertising campaign will depend upon using creative skills effectively and making the correct choice of media.

Media selection will also depend upon the target audience, that is, the number of **potential customers** the advertiser will wish to reach (**coverage**), as well as the number of times the advertiser wishes the message to be transmitted to customers (**frequency**). In order to plan a campaign an advertiser will need to gather detailed information about members of the target audience. Television stations will always provide information about demographic distribution, communications, size and nature of companies, spending patterns, leisure activities, incomes, etc. The coverage and frequency of media choice will then be limited by financial constraints; the advertiser must distinguish between those media which are affordable and those which are not. They will then aim to make a media choice on the basis of cost effectiveness.

For an advertisement to be cost effective, it must not only have good coverage but its frequency must produce the required impact upon the target audience. The **Threshold Concept** illustrates that unless advertising for a particular brand reaches a certain level it will be wasted. An advertisement's effectiveness will therefore relate to advertising expenditure; the number of times people are exposed to a message will help to determine whether they remember it.

Media coverage will help to create preferences for a product or service which could influence a purchase decision. It might also help existing customers to purchase more and reinforce consumer feelings that they have made the right purchase decision. It will allow organisations to develop a strategy, perhaps in response to competition, manage a brand and develop its market share.

Types of Media

Printed media makes up by far the largest group of media in the UK. It includes all newspapers and magazines, both national and local, including advertisers as well as trade press, periodicals and professional journals. There are about 9 000 regular publications in the UK which can be used by the advertiser. They allow the advertiser to send a message to several million people through the national press or to target magazines of special interest, from railways to snooker. They also allow the advertiser to communicate with people in a certain trade or profession as well as those in a particular region.

The printed media allows accurate targeting of promotions in customer segments, which can be identified by a **readership profile**. Long or complex messages can be sent and, as the message is durable, may be read repeatedly. If an advertisement appears in a prestige publication it may take on the prestige of that particular publication. Colour quality is today offered in an increasing number of newspapers and magazines; tear-off reply coupons which follow up an advertisement are also popular.

Advertisements in the printed media are sometimes criticised for having a poor impact. There are many competing messages which the reader is not forced to read. Ads are limited, and have static rather than dynamic qualities.

Broadcast media includes commercial television and commercial radio – the most recent addition being satellite television.

Broadcast media, especially television, is the most powerful media channel available. It reaches about 98% of households and viewing figures can exceed 20 million. The presentation quality of commercials is generally of a high creative quality, helped by both colour and sound. Messages are dynamic as they have voice, images, movement and colour and the ability to be repeated over and over again.

The main disadvantage of such an expensive media is that it is difficult to target a broadcast to a particular market segment; the message will not be relevant for many receivers. Radio in particular is seen as a background media. Remote control and videos also aggravate the problem faced by advertisers.

CASE STUDY ### The power of the media

Several years ago Kia-Ora was number three in the UK squash market and in danger of becoming unlisted by the major grocery chains, as the policy of stocking just two brands as well as own brands became widespread. At the time six retail multiples were tying up more than 50% of the squash market threatening Kia-Ora's volume and profitability.

Schweppes had a policy of having a strong brand in all sectors of the soft drinks market and so relaunched Kia-Ora in cheaper plastic bottles, redistributing money into advertising. The advertising agency BMP Davidson Pearce were briefed to achieve maximum impact quickly to ensure the trade would continue to stock the product and consumers would increase buying it. The agency produced two films positioning Kia-Ora as 'the one the kids want' and 'the one mums think their kids want.'

In the first twelve months of advertising, value and share increased by over 50% and Kia-Ora jumped to the number two slot in the market. By the end of the second year it had secured brand leadership. After paying for itself, the campaign proved to be highly profitable.

Task
Look at the case study and identify the success factors. Consider how an expensive campaign such as this could pay for itself and also prove to be highly profitable.

Outdoor media include fixed posters, hoardings, advertising on buses, taxis, underground trains and other forms of transport, as well as neon signs and electronic screens. It is particularly useful for providing frequency and supporting the images created through the broadcast media.

If outdoor media is well-sited, its impact may be considerable. Posters can be in colour and there is a wide choice of locations and sites with little competition from other advertising matter. In fact, many become a sole attraction where people have little to do except look at the advert or fellow-passengers.

Outdoor media suffers from the intrusion of noise and clutter from the immediate environment. Advertisements may become part of the scenery and go unnoticed. Outdoor posters are always subject to damage from vandalism and graffiti and many people today feel that hoardings intrude into the environment.

Direct mail involves establishing a direct relationship between the organisation promoting the product or service, and the customer. The advertiser supplies promotional literature to encourage a sale and then caters for customers' needs. It does not involve any of the normal intermediaries in a chain of distribution. It is generally recognised as the most rapidly increasing form of promotion as it allows a supplier to reach a narrowly defined target segment of a market from an up-to-date mailing list; promotional literature only reaches the market advertisers wish to contact.

The ability of direct mail to target precise market segments makes it cost effective, as it eliminates the supply of mailshots to those unlikely to buy. The majority of mailshots are read and organisations often use sales promotions such as offers and competitions to encourage a response.

If a good impression is made with the consumer, direct mail can offer organisations the opportunity to send a long message and some detailed copy. Organisations such as the Automobile Association, Reader's Digest and the National Geographic magazine are well established in using direct mail techniques. It is the most easy form of promotion to measure as it is possible to calculate the number of mailshots sent out, the cost of the campaign, the response rate and the number of sales made. Developments in computing and databases have enabled customer and market information to be broken down and stored easily on lists which may be purchased by organisations wishing to send out mailshots.

The Royal Mail offers a wide variety of services to help organisations make their direct mail cost effective. They point out to prospective customers that direct mail is the most selective form of promotion which has a very high impact compared with other advertising messages and enables an organisation to make personal contact with their customers. The Royal Mail offers a choice of service, a range of sizeable discounts and international services as well as the availability of the Business Reply Service and Freepost.

CASE STUDY ## Travel advertisers

British travel and holiday firms have discovered direct marketing and find it to be a good method of reaching their target market. Trusthouse Forte began to think that it had been spending a lot on above-the-line print without developing any relationship with customers. It started using **direct response marketing** to build product awareness and lasting relationships with clients. Butlin's Holiday Worlds also decided that it was cheaper to persuade existing customers to come back again rather than to recruit new customers. The company also felt that direct response adverts helped make early bookings and plan for the season ahead.

Travel firms are now learning to improve their customer targeting and to build up their databases. Club Med personnel felt that improved database marketing and appropriate investment will allow them to develop customer prospect files. P&O's Canberra Cruises see the need to target more mature, cash-rich clients for their holidays. The firm's staff thinks that above-the-line marketing will create the interest in their holidays and direct marketing will help them to follow up leads to generate customers.

Task 1

Explain why direct marketing has become an important method of selling holidays.

Task 2

What is meant by a database? Suggest methods a travel company could use to set up a database of potential users.

Cinema has been declining in numbers over recent years and today tends to be a medium popular with the young. It is therefore an appropriate way of targeting a younger audience and advertisements reflect this market.

The cinema has a captive audience; the sheer size of promotions and volume of advertisements makes them almost impossible to ignore. Then quality of both the sound and vision helps an audience to recall cinema commercials better than those on television.

Cinema audiences fluctuate widely and are dependent upon the popularity of the films being shown. Commercials are only shown once during a programme and are not reinforced as most young people are not regular attenders. Home-based entertainment has largely replaced cinemas and this has been helped by the spread of video recorders and the availability of films on cassettes.

Advertising effectiveness

Advertising is an essential part of the promotional mix and requires particularly large levels of expenditure. It is therefore crucial that organisations try to analyse the effectiveness of their investment. This is not always easy to do; it is difficult to see how advertising relates to market share unless an advertising campaign is curtailed.

The effectiveness of a campaign will depend upon the way it appeals to the attitudes of its target audience. Advertising will help to create stability in a market. Many customers are intensely loyal and expect to see promotional messages from advertisers of goods they regularly purchase. They often rely upon them for product information and for details relating to future purchases.

Advertising effectiveness will also depend upon how appropriate it is to its particular market segment. If it can be narrowed to a specific segment, it will yield the greatest results. Effective advertising might also help to influence the attitudes of its audience and the way the organisation is viewed by others.

The most common method of assessing the value of an advertising campaign is to test the views of a representative sample both before and after a campaign. Pre-testing will discover the customer's perception of a product before the campaign. Post-testing would involve asking the same questions to discover how far knowledge and understanding of the product had been improved.

Another method of assessing advertising effectiveness is through audience research to assess the reach and frequency of a campaign and its desired impact upon the target audience. Specialist agencies in the UK carry out audience research and their results are made known to advertising agencies, marketing departments and market researchers. British Rate and Data (BRAD) is the national guide to UK printed media. Its publications carry out readership research from areas such as specific market segments, socio-economic groups, business readers etc. Television Ratings (TVR) are carried out by the Broadcasters' Audience Research Board (BARB) on behalf of the broadcasting organisations. These statistics are also broken down on a demographic basis to indicate yields for specific age groups, socio-economic groups, etc. Commercial radio ratings are carried out by the Joint Industry Committee for Radio Advertising Research (JICRAR). A number of other specialist agencies provide advertisers with specialist information on types of advertising media, segmentation and audience composition.

Apart from advertising by direct mail, it is difficult to evaluate the effectiveness of an advertising campaign. One reason for this is because advertising is difficult to isolate from the benefits provided by the other ingredients in the promotional mix. Nonetheless advertising does have an important role to play and is essential for developing a market and stimulating sales.

CHAPTER 9

Sales Promotion, Personal Selling and the Role of Public Relations

Advertising is probably the most important controllable ingredient in the promotional mix. However, promotion requires other ingredients to support, complement and integrate with, the advertising function to ensure that an organisation achieves its marketing objectives.

Sales Promotion

Sales promotion describes a category of techniques which are designed to encourage customers to make a purchase. They usually complement advertising, personal selling and publicity and might include point of sale materials, competitions, demonstrations and exhibitions. The essential feature of a sales promotion is that it is a short term inducement to encourage customers to react quickly, whereas advertising is a much more long term communication process involving the building of a brand image.

Sales promotions can serve different purposes. For example, competitions, vouchers and trading stamps would be designed to build customer loyalty and perhaps increase the volume purchased by existing customers. **Product sampling** is a strategy which is often used to introduce new products into the marketplace. Clearance sales of overstocked goods will increase sales during seasons when business would otherwise be slack. Many sales promotions are undertaken in response to the activities of competitors to ensure that an organisation remains competitive. Oil companies, for example, offer competing promotional activities such as 'The Esso Collection' to encourage consumers to purchase their petrol.

There are two broad areas of sales promotions:

- those which are designed to enhance the sale and promotion of a product to the trade.
- those which assist the trade in promoting and selling products to the final consumer.

Selling into the pipeline is an expression often used to describe promotions which move products from the manufacturer into the distribution system. **Selling out of the pipeline** describes promotions which trigger the end-user to make a purchase.

Promotions into the pipeline

These are techniques used to sell more stocks into the distribution system. Though distributors will be impressed by promotional materials designed to encourage final consumers to make a purchase they will probably be more impressed by techniques addressed to themselves. These include:

Dealer loaders are among the inducements used to attract orders. They might include a 'free case' with so many cases bought. For example thirteen for the price of twelve is known as a 'baker's dozen'.

Point of Sale (POS) materials such as special displays, posters and racks can be offered against volume orders or offered on loan for a period. Some organisations might offer the use of a video recorder together with a promotional cassette to play for customers.

Dealer competitions might be linked to sales with attractive prizes for the most successful dealer.

Publishing of dealer names in advertisements, sales literature and in catalogues always encourages the support of the dealers.

Staff training is often provided for the dealer if the product involves detailed explanations, demonstrations or dealer servicing such as in the case of cars.

Extended credit often encourages dealers to stock goods, particularly if they receive payment for the product before they have to pay their suppliers.

Sale or return can be used to encourage a dealer to stock an untried product and helps to remove the danger of being left with unsold stock.

Promotional gifts such as bottles of spirits, clocks and watches sometimes influence the choice of goods dealers stock.

CASE STUDY — Travel and Tourism

Tour operators offer attractive sales promotion packages for travel agents, their managers and/or their counter staff. These often include gifts such as tour operators' travel bags, badges and pens, prize draws, money bonuses and competitions. In addition, in order to achieve the objectives of a particular sales promotion, a tour operator might offer an incentive commission of 2½% or more for achieving a particular sales target. It is also normal in travel and tourism for a distributor to be offered free travel to sample a holiday being promoted.

Task 1
Comment briefly upon the range of promotional incentives offered to travel agencies and their staff. Could you suggest any other promotional devices to use to encourage agencies to sell more holidays?

Task 2
Why do you think 'into the pipeline' promotions have developed in the travel industry? If you were a newly-formed tour operator, what rôle would sales promotions play in your overall marketing strategy?

Promotions out of the pipeline

These assist the trade in promoting and selling products for the end-user. Manufacturers tend to be responsible for the bulk of sales promotions though more recently retailers have started to become involved. Sales promotions to the end-user require a careful creative approach as repeated use, or a tasteless promotion, might damage a brand. Promotions might include:

Free sample or trial packs are either given to customers or sold to them at low prices to encourage them to try the product in the hope it might stimulate them to make a purchase. Colman's Mello & Mild barbecue mustard sauce was distributed in small cartons to thousands of households when it was launched, to encourage them to make a purchase.

Bonus packs offer the customer more of the product for the same price so they get greater value for their money. Beer and lager cans often offer 12½% more for the same price.

Coupon offers in the form of money off are often distributed from door-to-door, or appear as part of an advertisement or on a pack.

Price reductions are always popular with consumers but can prove expensive for manufacturers and retailers as many of those who buy the product might be regular users who would have been prepared to pay the full price for the product.

Competitions may interest a consumer particularly if there is an attractive prize. Scratch cards, free draws and bingo cards are often popular.

Premium offers may offer an extra product for the same price. They might offer a free gift with the pack such as the Frosties' moving holograms or the Rice Crispies' pencil top. Sometimes a promotion offers a free gift for a collection of tokens or packet tops; some require money as well as such proof of purchase.

Demonstrations at the point of sale which involve giving away samples or demonstrating a product often generate considerable interest. These tend to be expensive, however, and are often considered not to be cost-effective.

Trading stamps have largely disappeared from the retailing scene but are still used in petrol stations. A certain quantity of stamps is given every time a purchase is made and these can be redeemed later for goods or services. This helps to reinforce brand loyalty.

Charity promotions are often popular with younger customers. Customers collect box tops or coupons and when they send them to the manufacturer a donation is made to a charity.

Point of sale displays and merchandising are designed to push products to consumers from the location they are sold. Effective point of sale display attracts a customers' attention and encourages them to approach and inspect the product before making the decision to buy. **Merchandising** is the physical process of stocking goods so that they are in the right place at the right time and making it easy for the customer to walk around a store, select the goods they require and take them away. It provides a competitive advantage to the retailer by supplying products at the right eye-level and at a location relative to height. Look at the sweet and crisp displays in your local supermarket! It also involves providing access for the physically handicapped, the placing of own brands next to manufacturer brands so that prices can be compared and the siting of impulse items near to cash registers.

The effects of sales promotions

The effects of individual sales promotions will vary widely. Though most promotions such as free samples will clearly lead to an immediate increase in sales, on the whole sales promotions are a short term measure and have little effect on brand loyalty over a longer period. For the manufacturers of staple goods such as washing-up liquid and bleach, sales promotions will not affect market size which will be relatively fixed though they might encourage buyers to move away from competing brands. However, manufacturers of luxury products will be able to affect market size in the short term with promotional activity. The confectionery market is notorious for the way it responds to sales promotions – first we had the blue smartie and now the white smartie!

CASE STUDY

Sales promotions

Recent promotions:

- Green battery manufacturer Varta pushed its new mercury and cadmium-free batteries with two free giveaways – packs of garden seeds and a cassette head cleaner.

- Qualcast's most recent sales promotion revolves around a lawn care information pack for purchasers of Qualcast products.

- Midland Bank launched *Artscard*, its first affinity credit card. Every time the card is used, a percentage of the purchase will be directed by Midland to one of the beneficiary arts groups, many of which belong to the Arts Council.

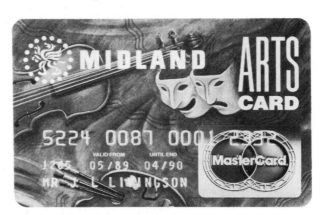

Figure 9.1
Midland Artscard (*Source: Midland Bank plc*)

- Rupert Murdoch launched an aggressive £2 million promotions pack through his *Today* newspaper to bolster the audience of satellite television. The move was a mass giveaway of satellite receiving equipment.

Task 1

Comment briefly on the nature of the sales promotions illustrated in the four mini-cases. For example, in terms of originality, potential success and inducement to purchase.

Task 2

Comment upon whether, in your opinion, each of the promotions illustrated was a good exercise likely to boost sales, or a bad idea likely to damage a products reputation – or neither.

Task 3

Consider the various 'out of the pipeline' sales promotions mentioned. Over a period of a week, make a note of examples which fit into each of the categories listed and then discuss your reactions to each of the examples you have obtained.

Personal selling

Every day of our lives we are involved in some form of **personal selling activity**. It might be persuading a friend to accompany you to a sports event or a relative to buy something for you. What you are doing is using a relationship to sell your ideas to someone else.

Personal selling involves persuasive communication between a seller and a buyer which is designed to convince the consumer to purchase the products or services on offer. The objective of personal selling is therefore to make the sale and is the culmination of all of the marketing activities that have taken place beforehand. It involves matching a consumer's needs with the goods and services on offer. The better the match the more lasting the relationship between the seller and the buyer.

The role of personal selling will vary from business to business. It can be one of the most expensive ingredients of the promotional mix. Though the high cost of salaries, commissions, travel and hotel expenses are a major disadvantage, personal selling is a two-way process of personal communication which allows an organisation to obtain information about its customers. This personal communication element can be very important as the final sale might come as the result of protracted negotiations.

Personal selling is important in both consumer and organisational goods markets. In consumer goods markets, advertising is often the driving force which has *pulled* a product through the distribution network so that most consumers know what they want to purchase. In organisational markets, the purpose of a sales force is to *push* the product through the market.

The mnemonic used to describe personal selling and the sequence of events it creates is known as the **five P's**:

- **Preparation** sales staff should be adequately trained and familiar with the product, customers, competition and the market.
- **Prospecting** identifying prospective customers, or **prospects** before selling takes place.
- **Pre-approach** learning about the projected customer.

- **Presentation** this involves active selling skills and will include the use of **AIDA** (see Chapter 8)
- **Post-sale support** following up sales helps to create repeat business.

Preparation

Selling in a highly competitive world means that preparation has never been as important. Though it has been said that sales people are born and not made, skills knowledge and training can improve everyone's performance. Training is designed to build upon a person's selling skills and to use their personal abilities and understanding to follow the psychological stages of the sales process. Product knowledge is vital as it allows feedback from the prospect's questions about the product's technical specifications, benefits and functions. Comprehensive records should be kept upon customers which can be updated after each visit. Keeping sales records enables the salesperson to respond exactly to each customer's individual needs. Knowledge of competitors and their products enables the seller to respond to queries about the relative merits and demerits of products. Good preparation improves the chances of closing a sale.

Figure 9.2
Personal selling

Prospecting

Identifying customers is a traditional rôle fulfilled by a salesperson. They must locate **prospects** customers before any selling can begin. Though sales staff will already have a list of customers or accounts, a salesperson will often have to carry out 'cold calling'. This involves visiting or telephoning an organisation that the business has not previously had any dealings with. Cold calling by sales representatives has unpredictable results and can be demoralising if there is a cold reception.

Alternatives to cold calling might be through the use of **canvassers** whose job it is to find potential customers and then pass on the details to the sales representatives. Sometimes it is possible to use independent agents to find customers. Working on a commission-only basis, agents may reduce the need for an organisation to employ as many sales representatives, particularly if there are a large number of low value accounts. Insurance is sold using agents.

Many organisations today use direct mail techniques to stimulate enquiries for sales staff to follow up. A good mailshot will make it clear what is on offer and help to initiate the selling procedure. A growing form of selling approach is through the use of the telephone. **Telemarketing** is often regarded as a fairly cost effective alternative to cold calling in person.

Pre-approach

It is often necessary to learn about a potential customer. This might involve finding out about the past history of transactions, if any, by researching records; finding out who they are dealing with and whether they have achieved access to a decision-maker as well as ascertaining the general needs and aspirations of the potential customer.

Presentations

These must be made on the basis of a strategy (see AIDA Chapter 8). **Probing** is quite important at this stage, in order to find out what the prospect's needs are and where their priorities lie. Once the salesperson has discussed what this is, they can try to match their product or service with their needs. This might involve elaborating on the product's advantages, concentrating on aspects such as savings in costs, design ingredients, perform- ance specifications, after-sales services, etc. During the presenta- tion, the salesperson must constantly evaluate whether the product is appropriate to the needs of the prospect. It is unethical to sell something to them that they might not need – although this often happens. The larger and more complex the order, the more complex the negotiations over the conditions of supply. Sometimes sales aids such as product demonstrations, samples and literature will help the process. The prospect may have a variety of objections to the purchase. These objections might be genuine, as a result of a misunderstanding and excuses. They might feel genuinely reluctant to make a commit- ment at this stage. Logical, well presented arguments and incentives may overcome such objections. Timing is crucial to closing the sale. A salesperson must look for **buying signals** which indicate that they are close to a decision and almost ready to put their signature on an order form and discuss the contractual arrangements.

Post-sale support

This stage involves following up the sale. Promises that might have been made during the negotiations will have to be met. If the salesperson guarantees delivery by a certain date, that date must be held. Contacting customers to see if they are happy with the product will help repeat buying and improve the supplier's reputation for concern for its customers.

CASE STUDY

Telemarketing

The idea of **telesales** was born in the US in the 1960s as a fast-action sales tool. When it came to the UK it failed to develop properly and established a poor reputation. This was the *first* generation of what is now known as **telemarketing**.

As more sophisticated telephone skills developed for research, account servicing and a less harsh form of prospecting and appointment setting, telemarketing was viewed as being more acceptable. Despite this, it was still reserved for short-term emergency campaigns and was rarely integrated with other direct marketing activities.

The *second* generation of telemarketing involved spending large amounts of time and money on an exercise which was proving to be a poor investment – much of the information needed already lay around in offices, on pieces of paper, in card indexes or in the field in the boots of sales representatives' cars. Potentially useful sales information was being wasted, opportunities were lost and more accurate targeting was made impossible.

From this muddle telemarketing's *third* generation emerged, with the aim of contributing to a computerised database which could then be managed and integrated as part of an organisation's overall promotional mix. Such information was to provide an opportunity to analyse the market and the position of competitors. It was to create a new and more powerful use of the phone to build, maintain and service accounts, whilst at the same time linking with other marketing activities.

Shell Oil's domestic heating operation deals with a small and dwindling market. Telemarketing helps it to identify precisely who uses oil-fired central heating and thereby manage its operations more efficiently and effectively. At Saab, they feel that by keeping information about purchasers in a database and using telemarketing, they have improved their monitoring abilities.

Task 1
Describe the differences between the three generations of tele-marketing. How would the third generation of telemarketing enable a business to improve the way it manages its affairs?

Task 2
Describe how telemarketing could be integrated with personal selling.

The sales force

Sales staff operate as an information link between the suppliers and their customers. As a result, personal selling involves a boundary rôle; being at the boundary of a supplying organis-ation and also in direct and close contact with their customers. The rôle is often not only one of selling but also one of interpreting the activities and policies of each organisation to the other.

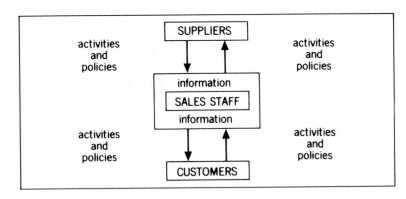

Figure 9.3
The information link between customers and suppliers

The size and nature of the sales force is determined by factors such as revenue and workload. Often large and widespread markets can only be supplied by a massive salesforce whereas small concentrated markets tend to make personal selling cost effective. No matter what other sales techniques are used in some markets, if customers become used to personal selling, they will tend to expect close contact with a representative from their suppliers. In these circumstances, particularly if a competitor uses personal selling, it can become very difficult to do anything but become locked in to the use of personal selling techniques.

Having decided upon the number of sales staff to employ, an organisation allocates its territories and, in doing so, tries to provide an equal work load for representatives. Salaries might be in the form of basic pay only, basic plus commission or commission only.

The rôle of personal selling has changed quite considerably in recent years. Despite improvements in database management, changing patterns of distribution and the concentration of purchasing power reducing the size of the workforce, personal selling will continue to play an essential rôle in providing buyers with goods, services and information to help them to manage their activities for a long time to come.

Public Relations

Public relations encompasses all of the actions of and communications from an organisation. The forces in an organisation's external environment are capable of affecting them in a variety of ways. The forces might be social, economic, political, local or environmental and could be represented by a variety of groups such as customers, shareholders, employees, special interest groups and by public opinion. Reacting to such elements in a way that will build a positive image is very important.

The purpose of public relations is therefore to provide an external environment for an organisation in which it is popular and can prosper. Building goodwill in such a way will require sound organisational performance and behaviour and the communication of such actions and attitudes to its many publics. Lord Mancroft once defined PR quite wryly as 'The art of arranging the truth so that people like you.'

The direct selling of products or services is not an objective of public relations. Whereas advertising is about relatively short term objectives, public relations is long term; it works by sending free messages to various groups through the activities the organisation undertakes in order to improve its reputation and maintain its positive image.

According to Frank Jefkins, public relations involves a transfer process which helps to convert the negative feelings of an organisation's many publics into positive ones.

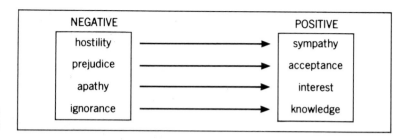

Figure 9.4
The PR transfer process

Public relations policy can be developed as a strategic device to provide an organisation with a competitive advantage. By *identifying* the unfavourable attitudes of interest groups and their influence over the external environment, an organisation can develop a PR *strategy* to create a more favourable attitude, to reduce the negative effects, and to build up a more positive perception and image. Public relations activities might include:

Charitable donations and community relations are good for an organisation's image, often provide lots of good publicity and also help to promote and provide for a good cause.

CASE STUDY   Red noses

Woolworths pulled off a publicity coup when they became the only major retailer to supply red noses for Comic Relief. In addition to footing the production costs of the rose-scented plastic noses, its high street stores have organised hundreds of fund raising events. At Woolworths' staff felt that Comic Relief provided an opportunity to add an extra dimension to their stores, and it certainly proved its worth. Store traffic inevitably increased and the noses attracted lots of children. The opinion was that it was a lot of fun for everyone involved.

Task 1
Explain how Woolworths' publicity coup to supply red noses would improve their image.

Task 2
How else would Woolworth's benefit from such a campaign?

Hospitality at top sporting events is a popular method used by organisations to develop their customer relations. An organisation called 'Sports Centre' provides an events booking service and boasts that they have 'something for everybody' by providing the opportunity to entertain customers at events like the F.A. Cup Final, Wimbledon, The Grand National and the Derby.

Press releases covering events affecting the organisation such as news stories, export achievements, policy changes, technical developments and anything that enhances the organisation's image are a useful form of public relations.

Press conferences are used to cover newsworthy events which are of interest to a wide variety of media.

Visits and open days are a popular method of inviting various publics to improve their understanding of what an organisation stands for. The Sellafield Visitors Centre claims to provide 'a window in on the nuclear world' and has become a top tourist attraction in the north-west of England.

Figure 9.5
The Sellafield Visitors Centre
(*Source: British Nuclear Fuels plc*)

Event sponsorship of sporting and cultural events is viewed as a useful oppportunity to associate an image with a particular type of function. For example, the Barclays League, the NatWest Trophy and the Embassy World Snooker Championship.

Corporate videotapes have become increasingly popular over recent years as a method of providing a variety of interested parties with information about company activities.

Minor product changes often take place in response to campaigns from consumer groups. For example, The British Union For The Abolition of Vivisection (BUAV) continually attack organisations which use animals in the testing of cosmetic, toiletry and household products. Tesco is one of many companies which have launched their own cruelty free ranges in response, and The Body Shop's reputation has been built almost exclusively on its eco-virtuous approach to bodycare products.

Magazines, publicity literature and education services, in both the private and public sector provide strong informed links between organisations and their various publics. For example, most organisations over a reasonable size will send out magazines and brochures in response to enquiries in order to indicate what their activities, functions, beliefs and objectives are.

- Shortly before Yorkshire Water was privatised in 1989 it sent all of its customers a booklet indicating the extent of its responsibilities.

- The Health Service sent all households in the country a booklet entitled 'The NHS Reforms and You' designed to inform and reassure potential patients.

- In the North-East of England, the Royal Mail sends households a booklet which provides up-to-date information on local postal services.

- Darlington Borough Council provides extensive promotional literature, some of which is printed in different languages.

- Large organisations such as BP, the Banks, British Rail, the Inland Revenue etc have their own educational services which supply packs of information and resources to schools.

Other public relations activities sometimes include clubs (the Severn Valley Railway recently set up a club for its younger users), staging of events, appearances on TV, awards, competitions, hot air balloons as well as anything which serves to maintain interest and support for an organisation's activities.

Figure 9.6
Launch of Junior Club with Jimmy the Jinty (*Source: Severn Valley Railway*)

Task 1

Make a list of up to ten public relations activities you have recently come across. Comment upon the effectiveness of each and then discuss your findings with your colleagues.

Task 2

Think of organisations which you feel need to improve their public relations. Suggest what public relations activities they could engage in and assess how effective they might be. Discuss your findings.

The framework for a practical public relations programme is a frequently used six point model. This provides:

1 appreciation of a situation/PR audit – the perception of the negative feelings of an organisation's publics

2 definition of PR objectives

3 definition of publics

4 PR techniques to be used

5 budget provision

6 assessment of results related to original objectives.

The continued existence of organisations is dependent upon the consent of their various publics to deal with them. The public relations function is therefore to create a favourable climate within this environment and to provide a positive perception of their activities. PR can be used for a variety of purposes. It can provide its publics with *information* about the organisation, what it does and how it responds to different circumstances. It can build *confidence* in its activities, develop *goodwill* in the community and provide *benefits* for its publics which might reach many who would not otherwise get to know of its activities. Public relations is just one function of an organisation's overall communications strategy designed to improve its image by helping to get the *message* across.

CHAPTER
10 International Marketing

The need to trade with other nations

In an interdependent world, international trade is an economic necessity. We are not self-sufficient and are therefore dependent upon the imports of raw materials and products from other countries. Exporting overseas helps to maintain our standard of living by making importing possible. Our relationship with other nations is under especial scrutiny at the moment, as 1992 will change our attitudes to brands, promotion and pricing.

There are marked differences between trading within a national economy and trading on an international basis. Each country has its own distinct economic identity, regulations, currency, standards and language which make it more difficult to trade between one state and another. Much of the opposition to the breaking down of barriers in Europe in 1992 stems from a cultural chauvinism which fears a loss of such identity. Though companies take on a lot when they decide to expand their horizons to other countries, they do so because international operations will provide them with further opportunities to develop than those within the domestic economy.

Companies trade overseas to achieve growth, particularly if the domestic market is static and mature. It can also allow them to use up their surplus capacity or to spread their investments. By expanding output they can then achieve greater **economies of scale**. This means that over a larger output, costs per unit are reduced and provide the supplier with a competitive advantage. It also means that in markets where competition has been dominated by suppliers who trade on an international basis, the only way to compete with them would be to trade internationally as well.

Opportunities overseas might arise in developing countries where the goods or services produced by organisations in more developed countries might be in demand. Sometimes available and economic labour forces and other economic benefits will exist in other countries that make it worthwhile producing there. Hong Kong and Taiwan have proved to be attractive places for overseas investment. Setting up manufacturing units overseas is sometimes called **economic imperialism**. Many of the goods and services we use everyday in this country are either from overseas or are produced by overseas subsidiaries which are household names in this country. For example, Ford, Procter & Gamble, Heinz and IBM are primarily American companies. British companies such as BP, ICI, Glaxo and British Airways probably have a similar effect in countries in other parts of the world.

International marketing therefore has a broad meaning. It is not just marketing of goods produced in one country to other countries. It also includes the development and management of business interests in other countries, which includes manufacturing, distribution and marketing systems. These activities may take the form of

- indirect exporting using export houses
- direct exporting overseas
- licensing, royalty agreements, franchising and other joint ventures with organisations overseas
- setting up wholly owned subsidiaries overseas.

CASE STUDY

General Motors into Europe

General Motors (GM), the world's biggest car maker, is planning a major marketing drive into Europe with the intention of re-establishing US built cars on the world market. It could bring famous car brands such as Cadillac, Chevrolet and Pontiac into the UK market in a big way.

The company plans to launch a slimmed down version of the US car range with the aim of achieving 100 000 unit sales per annum by the mid-1990s. At the Geneva Motor Show, GM presented the Corvette ZR1 as a showpiece to bury the misconception that US cars are just gas guzzlers.

Apart from its European manufacturing subsidiaries Opel and Vauxhall, GM has had only a small presence in the European market place. Sales reached a peak in 1979 with the sale of 32 500 US-built vehicles but in 1988 GM sold only 12 000 vehicles, 100 of which came to the UK.

GM is basing its ambitions on the fact that its cars now meet all European standards of emissions and economy. The American cars are unlikely to be sold through existing Opel and Vauxhall dealers but will be sold through an expansion of the company's Overseas Distribution Corporation. GM's greatest rival Ford is believed to be restrained by capacity from exporting significant numbers of cars to Europe.

Task 1
List the probable reasons why General Motors wish to export more US-built cars on the world market.

Task 2
Carefully consider what sort of barriers and difficulties exist for GM in European operations. Comment upon your findings.

Explain why GM are not going to sell their cars through the existing Opel and Vauxhall dealerships.

Task 3
How might GM's move affect its position with its greatest rival Ford?

Differences between domestic and international marketing

International marketing involves recognising that people all over the world have different needs. Organisations must accept that differences in values, customs, languages and currencies will mean that many products will only suit certain countries and that there is rarely such a thing as a **global market**, but rather a number of different foreign markets.

Catering for such differences involves greater risk. Developing products for different overseas markets and also being aware of the changes in currency prices requires careful **planning and research**. Difficulties are also likely to be encountered when competing with another nation's domestic producers in their own home territory as well as other organisations internationally marketing their products and services. No organisation can hope to be successful unless all of their key functions are **integrated** and developed so that the new and unfamiliar elements are effectively provided for.

Before trading overseas, an organisation must develop a thorough understanding of the country with whom they propose to trade. This must involve discovering their policies towards organisations overseas. The organisation will need to be clear about trade barriers such as tariffs or quotas which might restrict the flow of products across borders and the extent to which home manufacturers are protected against foreign competition. It will also require detailed knowledge of different legal and financial regulations required by the other country; this could involve employing specialist agencies to deal with the various bureaucratic requirements of such markets. Understanding the **marketing and distribution structures** is vital so that organisations can develop a strategy to sell their goods and services.

Consumer behaviour, culture and customs vary throughout the world. Patterns of demand will be determined by areas such as lifestyles, incomes, use of credit, family and religion. For example, exporting alcohol-based products to Islamic countries would be totally inappropriate. By understanding such influences an organisation can develop their product to make it more relevant to the inhabitants of a particular country.

Communication systems differ widely throughout the world. It may be possible to contact representatives easily in the capital of another country but not in other cities and towns. Such a lack of communication may make it difficult to control goods in transit or keep in touch with representatives and channels of distribution. Business activities require written and spoken communication which will influence promotional strategies, for instance, where there is a low level of literacy, television may be an important form of media. Language difficulties might also present a problem, particularly if several languages are spoken in the same country, and might involve employing multilingual staff.

Different economies

The ability to market overseas is dependent upon the capacity of organisations in the target country to *pay* for the goods and services they require. A country's economic well-being and guarantees of payment will play an important rôle. The use of different currencies makes the process more complicated. If payment from local currency is unacceptable, then trading will depend upon foreign currency reserves. Often, countries in the Third World cannot earn sufficient foreign currency to buy in goods and services to satisfy their needs. Counter-trading is sometimes an alternative whereby imports or goods are exchanged for other goods. For example, imports of cars might be exchanged for coffee. Recent developments in Eastern Europe have seen a marked increase in counter-trading.

Transactions overseas depend upon the **value of the currency** involved. Currencies are subject to fluctuations in their value against other currencies. For example, the relationship of the yen to the dollar may vary from one day to the next because of the changes in the demand and supply of the two currencies. If the pound falls in value, this makes British goods cheaper and this will then determine an organisation's income and therefore the probability of a transaction overseas.

Trading overseas will involve an assessment of **political risks and events** which might affect an organisation's activities. An unstable regime may create an environment which damages trade and results in a lost investment.

International marketing involves more than simply making products or services available to people in other countries. It requires an understanding of all of the areas mentioned and more. There may be **protocols** to follow, such as diplomatic channels or negotiations between senior managers and directors. Catering for an overseas market and all of its demands will involve considerable organisation to cope with such activities.

CASE STUDY

Lancashire into China

Lancashire Enterprises, the economic development agency for Lancashire, is in the process of building a Western-style business park in the City of Shenzhen in the Guangdong province of China. It has acquired a 55-year lease on a site with an option to extend. Lancashire Enterprises is hoping to offer mediating services to companies throughout Europe.

Relationships between Lancashire Enterprises and China go back twenty years to a student exchange programme. The agency's China Development Officer attributes their special relationship to good contacts at central and provincial government levels.

By using Lancashire Enterprises, companies can cut out several expensive visits to China and also learn about Chinese business etiquette and the lengthy procedures for trade agreements in China. The agency can use its contacts to analyse a business proposal to assess the likelihood of it succeeding before a company embarks upon the protracted bureaucratic process of setting up in China.

Task 1
Explain how Lancashire Enterprises have developed their relationship with the Chinese authorities.

Task 2
Discuss how Lancashire Enterprises can benefit organisations wishing to trade with China. Outline the difficulties they might otherwise face if they did not use Lancashire Enterprises.

Task 3
Comment upon why China would appear to be an attractive market for Western companies. To what extent do you think that Western goods would meet the needs of the Chinese peoples?

Indirect exporting

Many organisations first venture into the field of international marketing through an **export house**. An export house is not a manufacturer but an organisation whose main activity is the handling or the financing of export trade. Export houses have links throughout the world and play a prominent role in promoting exports and providing valuable knowledge and experience for manufacturers and suppliers. By undertaking this function, export houses enable organisations to enter overseas markets without having to invest in the costly financial and administrative procedure required to cater for consumers abroad.

For example, export houses can act as a **merchant** by buying in the home market and re-selling in the export market, and accepting the risks of loss in the search for profit. They may also act as a **manufacturer or supplier's agent** and hold the sole rights for the promotion and sale of products overseas on an agency basis. Export houses often act as an **export department** and market overseas in the name of manufacturers or suppliers and sometimes bear the credit risk. They might also act as a **buyer's agents** on behalf of an overseas buyer and, in doing so, accept responsibility for payment. Other specialist functions include acting as a **confirming house** and assuming responsibility to the organisation exporting for the payment of trade debts, as well as arranging **shipping**, **insurance**, **finance** and **credit** whenever required.

The export house helps to provide a well integrated link in the chain of distribution between the UK supplier and the foreign buyer and may act as a stockist or distributor. Doing so enables organisations to broaden their horizons without having to invest in specialist and costly administration and undertake the risk of exporting direct.

Direct exporting

Direct exporting involves manufacturers or suppliers shipping their products overseas and selling their wares directly to their customers using their own personnel. This might mean establishing **offices abroad**, employing staff to **monitor operations** and the constant study of overseas **trading restrictions**. This will require considerable investment in time, money and staff as, even on a limited scale, direct exporting will call for specialised administration of shipping procedures, freight and insurance rates, modes of transport, restrictions, licensing regulations, exchange control procedures, packing regulations and so on.

In the same way that the marketing environment has to be assessed at home, the overseas potential of markets has to be carefully scrutinised. Finding such information might be more difficult and mean that it takes longer to build up a knowledge of the territory. The potential market size, degree and type of competition, prices, promotional differences, product differences as well as barriers to trade have to be analysed alongside the cost effectiveness of various types of transportation. The organisation then has to assess the scale of the investment and consider both short and long term targets for an adequate return. A well-constructed strategy will enable them to identify the markets which offer the best financial returns and provide them with a careful assessment of the risks.

In order to cater for a different marketing environment, organisations have to consider a different marketing mix to the one used in the home market.

Before becoming involved in direct exporting an organisation must ensure that it is selecting the right product or service to sell abroad. In doing this it has to find the answers to two questions:

- Is there a market for the product?
- How far will it need to be adapted for foreign markets?

The product must possess characteristics that make it acceptable for the market – these may be features like size, shape, performance and even colour. For example, Red is a popular colour in Chinese-speaking areas but not in Africa. Many years ago, when Pepsi-Cola changed the colour of its coolers and vending equipment from a deep regal blue to light ice blue, the result was catastrophic in South East Asia, because in that part of the world, light blue is associated with death and mourning. Organisations also have to consider the differences arising from language, customs, health and safety legislation, labelling, packaging and safety standards. It might also be important to consider after-sales servicing guarantees and installation.

CASE STUDY   Procter & Gamble overseas

Staff at P&G felt that its business successes internationally have been through innovative product technology and marketing to local customers.

Crest Tartar Control was the first toothpaste clinically proved to reduce tartar build-up and prevent the risk of cavities between dental cleanings. There seemed limited prospects for marketing in Latin America because there is no Spanish translation for 'dental tartar'. However, consumer research showed that Latin Americans think of tartar as an ugly cement-like substance, expressed in their language by the word 'Sarro'. By calling the product Crest Anti-Sarro, the benefits of the toothpaste were conveyed and the message was delivered entertainingly by a celebrity opera singer.

When P&G entered the Japanese marketplace it found fierce price competition, complex government regulations, a sophisticated sales and distribution system as well as widespread cultural differences. This led to extensive research of Japanese society. For example, Japanese parents change their babies nappies more often than many other counterparts. They looked for better fit, comfort and less bulkiness. This led P&G to use technology to develop their product and led to ultra thin nappies. A successful introduction in Japan led to further distribution to other parts of the world.

- In India, P&G is studying ancient herbal medicines and traditions to produce natural products to treat many of today's common ailments.

- In the Phillippines, many people wash clothes with laundry bars and squeeze the juice of a local fruit, Kalamansi, into the water. Building on this information, P&G introduced Mr Clean Kalamansi and Perla Kalamansi.

- In certain Middle Eastern countries where it is not possible to reach women, consumer researchers rely on men for information about the products their daughters and wives require.

Tailoring products and strategies to markets has helped P&G products to become known and used around the world.

Task 1
Comment briefly on the way P&G has adapted their strategies to cater for markets in different parts of the world.

Task 2
What elements of the marketing mix needed scrutiny before entering the Japanese marketplace?

Task 3
What sort of requirement for overseas marketing does this case study highlight?

Factors in exporting
Pricing

Though **pricing policies** are as relevant whether the market is at home or overseas, additional circumstances have to be taken into account when exporting.

Freight and insurance costs, handling costs, costs of storage and customs duties all have to be considered, as well as any local taxes, trade margins and discounts. The price arrived at then has to be compared with the prices of competing products in that country. If the final price is higher than the competitors', the exporter will have to choose between certain options. For example, could designers trim costs, are accessories really necessary, could economies be made in packaging, presentation and promotion? Pricing must reflect international circumstances and the level of risk attached to the venture. It must also take into account the likely effect on revenues and profits of fluctuations in currency values.

Distribution

Getting goods to the right place through the channels of distribution was analysed in Chapter 7. Such analysis is as relevant to international marketing as it is to selling in the home market. However, export strategies for distribution will be much more complex. They might include the speed, type and time of transit, the effect of different climatic conditions on the goods during the journey, the extra freight, packing and insurance charges and differently structured distribution systems for consumer goods. For many companies, close analysis of distribution costs and techniques may provide a useful opportunity to develop an advantage over their competitors.

Promotion

Before planning a promotional campaign overseas, an organisation has to consider whether to use an advertising agency in the home country, subsidiaries of the UK agency or an overseas agency. The issue might hinge upon whether the exporter wants to keep close control over the agency's activities or whether they have full confidence in the overseas agent. Promotional activities in other countries may be completely different from those in the UK – there could be very few newspapers, television might only be for the privileged few and there could be many languages. The exporter will have to carefully investigate the alternative promotional media available and then develop promotional strategies appropriate to the culture of the inhabitants.

Having analysed their marketing mix, an organisation intending to export will look to both the government and other help provided for exporters. Britain contains only a small proportion of the world's population but is one of the world's largest trading nations. Considerable encouragement comes from the government for organisations to sell abroad. Much of this is co-ordinated by the British Overseas Trade Board (BOTB). Among the services provided by the BOTB are:

● **advisory groups** providing information on the world's main trading areas.

● **regional offices** providing a counselling service to meet the needs of individual organisations.

● a **market advisory scheme** and **overseas status report** service providing detailed information on markets.

● a scheme to provide technical help for exporters.

● assistance at trade fairs overseas where British firms can show their products.

In addition to these services, BOTB provides a daily computerised information service called the Export Intelligence Service (EIS) to help small and medium sized firms to enter overseas markets. It provides 50% of certain overheads for such ventures in the Market Entry Guarantee Scheme (MEGS) as well as publicity support for exports.

CASE STUDY The Queen's Awards for Export and Technology

1990 was an extra special year for The Queen's Awards for Export and Technology. It had been 25 years since the first Awards were made and a fitting celebration was planned.

● Each 1990 winner received a special plaque as a personal tribute of their success.

● In April, a set of four Royal Mail postage stamps was issued when the Awards were announced.

● The Design Council mounted a major exhibition.

The Awards are special in that they are given to a unit as a whole – both management and employees working together as a team. Winning The Queen's Awards brings prestige, credibility and often increased business. Recently, for example, a firm organising a joint venture in Saudi Arabia, needed references before signing a contract. When it was heard that the company had won one of the awards, the response was, 'Don't bother about references, let business commence.'

The Awards are valid for a five-year period and holders are entitled to fly the Award flag at their premises and feature the emblem on stationery, packaging and promotional materials.

Task 1
What do you think is the purpose of the Queen's Awards?

Task 2
How might winning such an award provide an organisation with a competitive advantage?

The Export Credits Guarantee Department (ECGD) is a government department whose primary function is to provide guarantees designed to encourage British exports of goods and services. It does this by providing attractive insurance rates against many of the risks of exporting, such as not being paid by customers in the event of insolvency, war, revolution, cancellation of UK export licences or delays in the transfer of sterling. The ECGD receives no subsidy from the taxpayer and has to operate on a commercial basis.

Some other sources of help and advice include The Central Office of Information (which operates an international information distribution service), international and overseas advertising agencies, public relations consultancies, BBC External Services and Universal News Services.

Licensing, royalty agreements, franchising

Licensing agreements

Market research might indicate that the most appropriate way to enter a market would be to arrange a **licensing agreement** with an overseas manufacturer. This would be the case if barriers to trade or excessive transport costs would otherwise make it impractical to export the goods. Licensing might involve an overseas organisation using another's patent, research, designs, trade marks and names. An organisation manufacturing under licence will often agree to pay **royalties** under the sales made.

Franchising

A similar sort of marketing strategy might evolve through **franchising**. Here a franchiser will provide a package of materials, expertise, advice and strategy for an overseas franchisee, who then provides services the overseas market with their own capital, enterprise and local expertise. The method allows a franchisee to use a well-established name or trade mark and enables the franchiser to spread their wares more quickly across markets whilst maintaining controls over the quality of their product or service. Payments are from royalties and contractual fees.

Contract manufacturing

Another type of joint venture might be through **contract manufacturing** where an organisation will seek a suitable manufacturer in a country overseas to arrange an agreement to produce their products there. Though the foreign firm manufactures the goods, the exporter may maintain control over the distribution and marketing. Often a UK-based organisation will purchase an interest in an existing foreign company or a UK company and an overseas partner will set up a new business enterprise together. The form of these types of agreements might be dictated by local company laws, traditions and policies. For example, local company law could prevent a foreign company from having a majority shareholding.

Wholly-owned subsidiaries

A company may employ a variety of methods to sell overseas. As it develops its markets through indirect exporting, it might start exploring direct, then set up some joint ventures and finally set up a **wholly owned subsidiary**. Such foreign subsidiaries might be used to market goods and services with depots and showrooms or may be as strategic manufacturing bases for either one or even a range of countries. Manufacturing overseas may enable orders to be met more quickly, reduce distribution costs and increase an organisation's overall competitiveness in overseas markets. Because such an operation requires considerable investment, it could lead to a high level of risk if the political situation is not secure. There has been an increasing trend for UK companies to set up subsidiaries in recent years.

CASE STUDY **H J Heinz Company**

H J Heinz is based in Pittsburgh, Pennsylvania, USA. It is a worldwide provider of processed food products and services. The company employs 39 000 people full-time, plus thousands of others on a part-time basis and during seasonal peaks.

Heinz products were first sold in Britain in 1886. Manufacturing in this country started in 1905 with the organisation of a small factory in Peckham. Today the Heinz group in Britain employs over 6 000 people and over 200 canned and bottled varieties bear the Heinz label.

Other long-established Heinz companies are in Canada and Australia. Since the war, Heinz companies have been established in Holland, Germany, France, Belgium, Portugal, Japan, Italy, Zimbabwe, China, Korea, Brazil, Thailand, Spain and Botswana.

Task 1

Explain what benefits an American company such as Heinz will receive from having manufacturing operations in so many different countries.

Task 2

Obtain promotional information from a company. Find out how it markets its goods or services overseas.

As overseas operations develop, companies achieve the status of **multi-national corporations** with production facilities in many countries and a head office in a parent country, as illustrated by the Heinz case study. Organisations like Ford produce Ford Sierras in Belgium but components are built throughout the European Community and the US. For instance, body assembly takes place in Belgium, but transmissions are made in England, France and Germany, electrical systems in Wales and England, axles in Wales and West Germany and engines in the US and West Germany. The success of the final assembly and the livelihoods of those involved depends upon detailed planning, delivery from suppliers through the EC and the US, skill-sharing and international co-operation. As the size of such operations have considerable economic power and their ownership and control crosses national boundaries and can have a profound effect upon a nation's welfare, governments closely monitor their activities.

The single market

The objective of the single 'common market' goes back to the original Treaty of Rome (1958). Despite the absence of tariffs and quotas between member states in the EC, the common market has not been a reality and there are still considerable differences between domestic and international marketing. For example, the free movement of goods has been affected by problems transporting goods across borders. A competitive market for services has been blocked by national restrictions. The operation of the market has been distorted by public purchasing policies and subsidies which have distorted the ability of producers throughout the EC to compete on the same terms. The idea of the single market was to remove barriers and thereby reduce business costs, stimulating efficiency and encouraging greater interaction across boundaries.

Progress towards the single market started in 1985 with a programme of action, the Single European Act, to remove all obstacles and distortions to trade by the end of 1992. This has meant that progress towards a vast package of measures and laws has had to take place. Areas covered include standards, testing, certification, medical products, public purchasing policies, broadcasting agencies, financial services, information technology, insurance, movements of capital, transport policies, company law, establishment of the professions, food hygiene, competition policy etc.

The EC comprises a community of over 300 million people – very nearly as many as the US and Japan combined.

It is the UK's largest export market comprising 50% of UK's total exports. The advent of the single market will provide new opportunities for UK producers to prosper in a more healthy business environment.

Harmonising brands

Today it is no longer possible to buy a Marathon chocolate bar. The UK's fourth favourite chocolate bar has been renamed Snickers. The reason for this has been to fall in line with Mars' global branding strategy as Snickers was known in every market except the UK.

Many other companies are harmonising brands across Europe. For example, Unilever's Radion is now identical in most European markets. Such global branding allows economies of scale, enables production to be standardised and saves on advertising costs because the same images can be used with different words.

Today greater care needs to be taken when establishing new brands to ensure they have the potential to be successful on an international basis. Denmark's Plopp chocolate would probably not be well received in this country. Apparently Fairy Liquid would raise eyebrows in the US and Irish Mist liqueur has a problem in Germany where mist translates to manure! A brand name is therefore something which cannot be ignored. In a recent survey across Europe IBM – an American company – was judged to have the most successful pan-European identity ahead of Philips, Mercedes-Benz and Shell. This is probably because IBM is rarely thought of as being American and is seen as local wherever they are sold. Modern companies are increasingly aware of the need to develop **core brand values** to meet common needs in all of their main markets.

Task 1
Make a list of brand names which you feel have a truly pan-European identity. Compare your list with those of others in your group.

Task 2

Choose two brand names you would consider not to be suitable for an international market. Explain why you consider that they fail to have 'core brand values'.

You don't always have to go overseas to export – the Lygon Arms in Broadway won the Queen's Award for export by marketing itself overseas and attracting a huge amount of visitors to the UK. In the leisure-conscious society, tourism and travel have become huge growth areas and need to be marketed as much as any more 'tangible' product.

11

Responsible Marketing

In a modern community, staying in business and meeting the expectations of shareholders is recognised as the major consideration affecting the actions of most profit-seeking organisations. But such organisations operate in a far wider environment which, as we saw in Chapter 2, entails an awareness of areas such as social, political, economic and environmental influences. In the same way that an organisation has to be aware of these numerous interdependent factors, it must also accept basic obligations to many of them in order to provide a more healthy and prosperous community in which all parties can co-exist. **Responsible marketing** should therefore involve good citizenship which facilitates an ethical approach to areas such as consumerism and environmentalism as well as to society as a whole.

Part of the problem, however, is that the activities that organisations engage in, and the decisions they take, often have conflicting interests which create both benefits and costs for those directly and indirectly affected. Today it is increasingly recognised that developments can only become socially effective if they take into consideration community losses as well as profits. This leaves many organisations with the decision as to where to strike a balance. Developing goods and services, building more factories and providing better roads may mean more jobs and wealth creation but at the expense of how much pollution and loss of farmland? What actions should an organisation take to compensate for such a loss?

CASE STUDY

The decline of the UK tobacco industry

The market research group Euromonitor recently predicted that the £6 billion tobacco industry faces total extinction within 30 years. For example, over the next three years cigarette sales are predicted to drop 10%. The report's editor feels that tobacco smoking is today viewed as anti-social but the tobacco industry does not seem to have faced up to the facts.

Euromonitor heavily criticises manufacturers for being far too concerned about Far-Eastern markets which are still growing to consider their UK crisis where retailers are becoming increasingly disenchanted with the poor returns from cigarette sales.

Some companies have responded to changing trends. Nabisco have diversified away from their tobacco interests in Winston and Camel, into other markets, such as breakfast cereal production,.

Task 1
Make a list of both the costs and benefits of the tobacco industry for the UK.

Task 2
Make a brief statement comprising your view of the activities, ethics and importance of the UK tobacco industry in the past, and for the present and future.

Task 3
Comment upon the strategy UK tobacco firms should be adopting to combat their rapidly declining market.

Consumerism

Prior to the 1960s, consumers had few rights and very little say in the bargaining process. They often had to rely upon their own common sense. The Latin expression *caveat emptor* – 'Let the buyer beware' – held true. As large and well-developed organisations often dealt with individual consumers, **consumerism** developed to break down this vast inequality in bargaining power and so provide consumers with more rights and enable them to obtain greater value for money.

The need for consumers to be better protected and therefore insured against the actions of the organisations they bought from arose because of areas such as:

● poor quality or damaged goods or services

● goods or services which fail to match the description applied to them

● manufacturer's or supplier's negligence affecting the safety of the product or service

● breach of contract

● misleading offers, information, advertising, labelling

● unfair terms in contracts

● monopoly control or lack of competition limiting the quantity and/or quality of a product and resulting in artificially high prices.

Greater quality, freedom of speech, improved educational standards and vastly improved communications in a rapidly changing and more technological world increased sensitivity about the rights of consumers. Consumers expected a product to be safe and perform its function well. They also considered it important that they were protected against questionable products or unfair practices and expected producers to behave in a socially responsible manner. This change in views, expectations and attitudes about the actions of manufacturers and producers helped to result in an extensive programme of consumer legislation.

In response to the consumer movement, many manufacturers or suppliers paid greater attention to the concept of the **total product**. The total product includes accessories, a handbook, a brand name, a user guarantee, packaging, after-sales service and a dynamic approach to quality. They felt that quality, attention to detail and providing for the total product would help to improve customer satisfaction and also maintain a good public profile. It would also help an organisation to reflect how it bears its responsibilities to the community at large. Such an approach not only benefits consumers, but also becomes an additional part of an organisation's marketing mix and provides them with a useful competitive advantage. Some organisations go further to proclaim excellence at the foundation of their corporate objectives. Glaxo talks about 'backing excellence, staying top.' General Accident has a corporate identity outlined by the slogan, 'Service – our foundation and our future.' They believe that quality becomes everybody's business from the most junior member of their staff to the most senior member of their management team and should permeate every area of their activities. They feel that quality and an organisation's success are directly related.

CASE STUDY The 'secrets' in the service

From humble beginnings, Wanes has become one of the North East's most successful motor retailers. One of the major factors contributing to this success has been the provision of extremely high standards of service which are unequalled elsewhere and have resulted in their excellent reputation for overall customer satisfaction.

Wanes Customer Service Programme claims unique and demanding high standards which it is thought to have been instrumental in retaining customer loyalty and have led to repeat purchases and recommended business. Staff are encouraged to build relationships based upon trust, respect and service and are viewed as the lifeblood of the business. Recently, with the customer in mind, Wanes undertook a massive redevelopment and building programme to improve staff facilities and the working environment at their Bishop Auckland, Catterick, and Northallerton branches and have just opened a designer-built garage in Hartlepool. These investments are part of an overall strategy. Though the investment has been immense the most important aspect was to employ the right calibre of staff 'to ensure that the high standards of service every customer receives and experiences are maintained.'

At Wanes there is no problem too small to handle. Customer participation is continually sought in pursuit of excellence with regular questionnaires, direct mail and telephone surveys undertaken throughout the year. The company no doubt feels that their 'secrets' are in their service.

Task 1
Explain why management at Wanes feel that quality and excellence have contributed to the success of their activities.

Figure 11.1
Providing a service *(Source: Wanes Garages)*

Task 2
Comment upon how the firm could control the quality of its activities.

Task 3
Look for an organisation which makes a claim about the quality or excellence of its goods or services. Examine how such claims and consequent actions enable that organisation to gain a competitive advantage over its rivals.

Consumer protection

The legal system provides a framework within which transactions can take place and also serves to provide a means of settling disputes. The legal basis of the contract which exists between the buyer and the seller sets out the obligations that individuals and organisations have to each other every time they enter into an agreement.

Over the years governments have responded to consumerism with successive **Acts of Parliament** designed to protect and increase the powers of buyers in relation to sellers. Such laws cover unfair business activities, poor quality of goods and services and the provision of credit. For example the Sale of Goods Act of 1979 indicates that sellers must provide goods which are of merchantable quality, match the description applied to them and are fit for the purpose for which they are sold. Other important Acts include the Trade Descriptions Acts of 1968 and 1972, the Fair Trading Act of 1973, the Consumer Protection Act of 1987, the Consumer Credit Act of 1974 as well as Acts referring to Food and Drugs and Weights and Measures. The legal aspect of marketing also covers areas such as agency, use of trade marks, infringement of copyrights, insurance, company law.

Often government actions create a range of organisations or departments designed to represent consumer groups. For example, the **Office of Fair Trading** investigates monopolies and mergers, collects information on unfair consumer practices and plays a key rôle in developing consumer legislation.

The Director General of Fair Trading:

- analyses information affecting the economic or health and safety interests of consumers.
- refers matters to the Consumer Protection Advisory Committee.
- encourages the publication of Codes of Practice for dealing with consumers.
- takes action against organisations which persist in conduct which is against the interest of consumers.
- provides a vast range of publications to cater for different consumer needs.

Another body is the **Advertising Standards Authority**, an independent body which exercises control over all advertising except that on radio and television. The Authority draws up its own codes which it uses to ensure that advertisements are 'legal, decent, honest and truthful.' Advertisements should be prepared with a sense of responsibility to both consumers and society and conform to the principles of fair competition. For example, a number of complaints were made to the ASA over a campaign by Rover to extol the virtues of wood panelling on the Rover 820 Se. Suspended by the main body of the text appeared a box with the words 'A woman, a dog and a walnut tree, the more you beat them, the better they'll be.' At Rover they insisted that the ad was only put there to inject humour!

The ASA were unconvinced of the cholesterol-reducing properties of the showpiece launch of Common Sense Oat Bran Flakes and brought in a team of top nutritional scientists amidst fears that the product and the ad might create needless worry for consumers.

Figure 11.2
Investigating complaints *(Source: The Advertising Standards Authority)*

The **British Standards Institution** was incorporated by Royal Charter as a voluntary non-profit making organisation to prepare and publish standards for safety, performance, size and testing. They are identified by the now-famous kitemark displayed on the product's packaging to denote that it meets

BSI requirements. During 1989 the first British Standard on major product design was published. This standard was part of the Government's drive to improve marketing effectiveness through design.

The **Monopolies and Mergers Commission** investigates possible monopolies and proposed mergers referred to it by the Director General of Fair Trading. Its rôle is to assess whether such monopolies and mergers are likely to be against the public interest. For example, during 1989 the MMC published their report on brewing. This report provided quite a headache for the 'big-six' brewers which have come to dominate the industry. Under the recommendation, brewers would not be allowed to own more than 2000 pubs which could force them to put up to 22 000 outlets on the market or could result in them selling off much of their beer-making capacity.

Trading Standards or Consumer Protection Departments are departments of local authorities which work with the Office of Fair Trading and help to enforce laws, offer advice for shoppers and traders and watch for unfair trade practices. There is also an extensive network of Citizens' Advice Bureaux in the UK which provides advice on consumer complaints and queries.

Another government established body is **The National Consumer Council**, set up in 1975 to provide independent advice to government and business organisations. It also seeks to further consumer interests by representation on public and other bodies as well as oversee the development of voluntary codes of practice. Nationalised industries have **Consumer and Consultative Councils** to influence their policies and ensure that they do not abuse their powers.

Consumerism has also led to the formation of a number of influential pressure groups and movements.

The Consumers Association has over 700 000 members and is the largest consumer organisation in the country. *Which ?*, its magazine, carries the results of extensive product tests and scrutinises services.

The National Federation of Consumer Groups comprises a large number of Local Consumer Groups which concentrate upon local issues such as retail facilities and prices. Other pressure groups which might aim to influence businesses and the government include ecological lobby groups, sports organisations, women's groups, the RSPCA, the Campaign for Real Ale, etc.

There is no doubt that when consumers' rights and obligations are abused or when dangerous goods are brought into the market place, feelings tend to run high. The media, through TV programmes such as *That's Life* and *Watchdog* and the radio and press have become an increasing focus for consumer campaigns.

In response to consumer pressures and increasing concern about the quality of goods and services, organisations in a number of industries have formed **trade associations** which have established **codes of practice** to go beyond the basic legal requirements and to provide the highest possible level of consumer satisfaction. For example, the Association of British Travel Agents sets up a fund to protect holidaymakers if a company fails to deliver. Other codes of practice apply to areas such as cars and car repairs, shoes and shoe repairs, electrical goods and servicing and mail order trading. Many of these codes have been produced by consulting with the Office of Fair Trading.

The **Chartered Institute of Marketing** has its own Code of Practice which members are required to adhere to as a condition of their membership. The code refers to professional standards of behaviour in securing and developing business and demands honesty and integrity of conduct. The **British Code of Advertising Practice** is supported by advertisers, agencies and the media whose representatives make up the Code of Advertising Practice Committee. The Code sets out the rules which those in the advertising industry agree to follow and also indicates to those outside advertising, the regulations designed to ensure that advertisements can be trusted.

Voluntary and statutory controls and the formation of active and strong pressure groups which often gain popular support from the media have helped to develop a changing climate for marketing activity. Organisations today can no longer disregard groups of consumers or wider environmental issues in which they should be involved and have to show greater sensitivity to their many publics.

CASE STUDY   Turning Green

The preservation of the earth is foremost in the minds of many consumers at the moment. In response to the increasing environmental movement many sections of industry have been in pursuit of the new breed of 'green' customer.

Though the 'greening' of industry is a positive development, a problem has arisen with some businesses and advertisers who want to be seen on the green side of the fence and, in doing so, fail to check the factual accuracy of their claims. For example, one car manufacturer claimed that a model designed to use unleaded petrol was as 'ozone friendly as it is economical'. Many would assume that this means that running on unleaded fuel does not damage the earth's ozone layer. Having made a purchase on the basis of this, a new car owner would probably be embarrassed to learn that lead is too heavy to reach the stratosphere and has absolutely no effect upon the ozone layer!

Other industries are turning green in response to increasing concerns. In the soap industry, Ecover and Ark have launched a range of ecologically-sound household products. The government have urged manufacturers to scrap the use of chlorine-bleached pulp in consumer products which could affect teabags, filters, toilet rolls and milk cartons. Such pulp has been linked to health risks because of the dioxin it contains.

Peaudouce claims to have introduced 'the friendliest nappy on earth' which does not contain chlorine-bleached fluff pulp. It also claims to have produced the UK's first biodegradable disposable nappy which has an additive to hasten the destruction of the plastic backing. According to Friends of the Earth, disposable nappies will never be green as the plastic needs the right conditions to break down and nappy manufacture requires huge amounts of trees.

Pressure has been mounting on the Government to produce a nationally recognised green label to identify environmentally friendly products. In West Germany, the Blue Angel is used on thousands of products. Many feel that the present situation confuses consumers. Meanwhile *The Green Consumer Guide* by John Elkington and Julia Hailes provides consumers with plenty of advice and its authors are now providing a consultancy service to advise companies on how to market green products.

Task 1
Comment upon your experience of claims which have been made about green products and say how truthful and accurate you feel these claims to be.

Task 2
Visit a supermarket and make a list of products which claim to be environmentally friendly.

Task 3
Express your opinions of a nationally recognised green label. What other controls could be introduced to add respectability to green claims?

Environmentalism

The environmental lobby works hand-in-hand with the consumer movement to provide protection against some of the excesses of the industrial and commercial world. They serve to remind firms that not only do they have internal costs but also external costs which go beyond their balance sheets. These costs are sometimes known as **externalities** or **spillover costs**.

Externalities = social costs − private costs.

At the end of the day, organisations will probably be more interested in weighing up decision-making using private costs, but will be forced to assess the fuller implications in order to use resources in a more socially acceptable way.

Pollution

The most obvious social cost of business activity is **pollution**. Many industrial plants choose locations near canals, rivers and the sea so that they can not only use water in the manufacturing process, but also pour out effluent into the rivers and the sea. In some countries, firms are charged heavily for causing water pollution.

Air pollution was highlighted by several horrifying events of the 1980s. In December 1984, the leak of poisonous gas from the Union Carbide plant in Bhopal, India, killed more than 2000 people and at least ten times that number suffered from severe respiratory and eye complications. Even more dramatic – and potentially catastrophic – were the events at the Chernobyl nuclear reactor in Russia in 1986 where wide tracts of land were made uninhabitable and a cloud of nuclear waste was carried airborne across Europe by the release of nuclear material. Emissions from UK plants are recognized as a major contributor to acid rain which has devastated forests in Scandinavia and Germany – half of the Black Forest has been designated 'a total damage area'.

The industrial response to environmental issues

Dereliction, traffic congestion, long term waste and noise are other external effects of business activities which influence the wider environment and determine how organisations are perceived by various parties. At the same time businesses have to consider the products. What use should they make of additives? How should the products be tested? Should animals be used in the tests? What use is to be made of wood and plastics? The more an organisation analyses environmental issues, the more it is likely to be faced by competing interests.

Internally the business needs to make a profit for shareholders who have to be content with the way the organisation is run. Externally they have to contend with having to sell products in the face of competition as well as the regulatory influences exerted upon them by governments and the pressures from a variety of other interdependent factors. Failing to take heed of organised pressure groups such as The Consumers Association, the National Anti-Vivisection Society, Friends of the Earth and so on may lead to the worst possible outcome – a consumer boycott.

In today's more discriminating world, many consumers are genuinely concerned about whether or not dolphins are killed in tuna fish nets or that products are green or cruelty-free. In fact many consumers develop a sense of purpose and satisfaction at making a contribution to improve the world they live in. Some organisations even try to run a counter-campaign to win public support. 'Come to Sellafield. Look around the place. See for yourself how safe it is.' This has been the multi-million pound message of an advertising campaign commissioned by British Nuclear Fuels PLC.

One of the strongest arguments today is for organisations of all disciplines to become involved in conservation. Modern businesses today depend upon non-renewable resources where only a limited stock exists. Many are worried about how they are being used up. Businesses tend to have been more concerned with short term profits than with the future of the world as a whole. In many areas of production and waste disposal, there are opportunities to use non-renewable resources sparingly and to recycle renewable and non-renewable resources. For example, there is a strong case for recycling glass on both environmental and financial grounds. Recycled glass melts at a much lower temperature than the raw materials of new glass. Less energy is required to collect, process and deliver the glass from a well-organised recycling scheme than to produce and deliver an equivalent amount of raw materials. To make 1 tonne of new glass requires 12 tonnes of raw materials, or just 1 tonne of broken glass (known as **cullet**). In all, each tonne of cullet added to the furnace means savings of about 30 gallons of fuel oil.

CASE STUDY

Caring for the world they serve

Increasingly, large organisations wish to be seen to be caring for the world as responsible citizens. Doing so is not only considered to be vital everyday practice but is also viewed as an investment in an organisation's future.

British Airways considers itself to be such an organisation.

- BA has one of the largest ground fleets in Europe and, wherever possible, all vehicles have been converted to lead-free petrol.

- An energy conservation programme has been established. The 747 repainting facility recently received a British Gas award for its efficient use of energy.

- In the Engineering Department, efforts are made to tackle issues such as the use of halon sprays and the disposal of chemical waste.

- Catering teams have made a conscious move towards reusable items.

- The British Airways Nature Conservation Initiative has been applying resources to help in the preservation of threatened animal and bird species, often by providing transport between their natural habitats.

Recently British Airways appointed a manager at executive management level with wide experience of environmental issues. With the adoption of an agreed policy for environmental matters, recognition of this responsibility now appears as one of British Airways seven corporate goals. At the moment they are carrying out a review of activities which involve aircraft noise, congestion around airports and aircraft emissions at high altitude. Besides identifying issues they are looking for solutions; to foster the enthusiasm of staff they have introduced a 'Greenwaves' category in the staff suggestion scheme.

This environmental focus is not simply designed to develop a trendy green image. It is viewed as part of British Airways overall approach to total quality in all their activities.

Task 1
Describe the possible costs and benefits to British Airways and its many publics of having an environmental corporate goal and of developing an environmental strategy.

Task 2
Working in groups, discuss and note your findings on how the organisation you work for or attend could develop a strategy to become more environmentally aware.

Marketing ethics

Ethics are **moral principles** or **rules of conduct** which are generally accepted by most members of a society. An ethic is therefore a guide as to what should be done or what should not be done. It involves what one believes to be right and what is considered to be wrong. From an early age, parents, religions and society in general provide us with moral guidelines to help us to learn and form our ethical beliefs. Many ethics are reinforced in our legal system and thus provide a constraint to business activities, while others are not. In areas not covered by law, pressure groups often form to put forward their case.

Through the media we often hear about both successful and questionable business activities. Issues such as insider trading, animal rights protesters involved in disputes with organisations producing cosmetic and pharmaceutical products, protests about tobacco sponsorships and trading links with nations such as South Africa are common news stories. As a result, consumers have become increasingly aware of both the ethical and moral values underlying business decisions. Today's consumer is more concerned than ever before about what the organisation whose product or service they buy stands for, who it trades with, what it does, whether it has political sponsorships, is seen as an equal opportunities employer and how it behaves in the community as a whole. For example, when *Which*? carried out a survey, 63% of responses were concerned about the activities of companies they might invest in.

The idea of organisations working in and for the community is not new. Many of the great entrepreneurs of the past such as William Hesketh Lever took action to support such beliefs. M&S contribute to a programme which they claim touches all areas of the community. It includes contributions to 'health and care' with involvement in projects for the elderly, the mentally ill and handicapped, the abused, to hospitals and *Childline*. It also includes contributions to 'arts and heritage' as well as 'community services, education and training'.

Health and safety is an area which has come to the forefront of company policies over recent years. Accidents on a chemical plant or in the North Sea can permanently tarnish an organisation's image. There is always the example of the American corporation which discovered that it was more cost efficient to pay compensation to ill, injured and dying employees than to invest in research to improve safety. At the same time, organisations have become increasingly aware of the adverse effects their products can have on the health and safety of consumers. A recent report attacked standards in the food industry and called for government to fund better research, better training for environmental health officers and to legislate against farmers who produce infected stock. Food scares such as the egg scandal, salmonella, listeria and 'mad cow disease' (BSE) shocked consumers and have seen sudden short term changes in demand. Cancer links with the use of chlorine bleach recently rocked the paper industry.

Buying cheap imports from 'sweat-labour' overseas, Sunday-trading, dumping of goods on foreign markets, the need to invest in areas of high unemployment, contribution to political parties, encouragement of trade unions, treatment of employees, investment policies, pension and insurance schemes, social clubs etc. The list of issues facing industry is almost endless. No organisation is ever going to be able to give the sort of response to these pressures that will please all parties all of the time. However, by becoming good corporate citizens and being socially responsible for their actions organisations can generate considerable goodwill and develop a useful marketing advantage whilst, at the same time, pursuing their other business objectives. However, many environmentalists would argue that being 'green' is not an option extra but a vital — and tardy — step to preserve the future of humankind.

There is no doubt that in the future, in the world of the articulate consumer we will see more 'social' marketing linking consumer, environmental and ethical issues. For example, Ark, the environmental group, which as part of its activities markets environmentally responsible products concentrates its activities upon the individual and how each person can make a positive step to restore the health of the planet. By doing so they hope to make people aware that everyone has an impact upon the environment and that if we endanger the planet's health by our activities, our own health will be at risk. Ark carries out its work by establishing a network of local groups, educational publications to provide them with information, celebrity endorsement and environmentally-responsible consumer products. Such products provide the consumer with choice, educate individuals about environmental issues, show their potential to the industry and increase consumer awareness of their impact upon the natural world.

In the future, organisations will have to respond with increasing sensitivity by constantly analysing their activities and revising their strategies to match the wishes of their customers. Many consumers will be willing to pay more to support a principle or even forfeit something they want in the short term in pursuit of a more permanent belief. Customer care, the pursuit of quality, an efficient public relations function, the running of educational services, image-building and responsible actions will help to get the message across. Such marketing will be more dynamic and require a better understanding of all the various constraints upon an organisation's behaviour.

CHAPTER
12
Marketing Planning

Making strategic decisions and setting objectives

Before you make a marketing decision you should set out the objectives that you are seeking to achieve. Strategy is very important to tell you where you are going and set out benchmarks against which you can evaluate your performance.

The ease with which you can set out clear objectives depends on the nature and timescale of the decision. For example, it is easier to set clear-cut objectives for short term operational decisions than for long term strategic marketing decisions. This is not surprising because the effects of long term decisions will be experienced over a long period of time. Strategic decisions will need to be modified as circumstances change. In contrast, the short term environment in which a business operates will be more stable and consumer actions will be more predictable.

Strategy involves setting out long term objectives. For example, a company may decide that the path to profit and growth lies in positioning itself in the upmarket segment of a high quality consumer product market. This general long term strategy can then be used as a broad guide against which more precise short term tactics and operating decisions can be set. For example, day-to-day planning can be set out in relation to the development of new product lines, and the development and modification of existing lines.

Strategic management should involve the setting out of corporate objectives for the total enterprise. An important part of this is to carry out a **strategic audit**, to find out what has been achieved in the past, and what can be achieved in the future. Management should set out to create a balance between resources and opportunities. Marketing should play a key part in this strategic process, because as we have seen, the key function of marketing is to keep the business in tune with the market place and hence the consumer.

CASE STUDY

Learning from the Japanese

The process of **simultaneous engineering** gives us an important insight into how a company can plan for success in the market place. Simultaneous engineering is simple but brilliant. In the West, many products are created by what is called **sequential**

engineering. Products are dreamed up, designed and then handed to the marketing department. The production engineers calculate how to make them, the suppliers gear up to produce the components, and, finally, the manufacturing department starts production.

At the first attempt, they usually find components do not quite fit together, that the tooling needs rejigging, or there is some other problem, and time is lost sorting it out. It is an exhausting process. As a result, the period from a product's inception to the point when it starts rolling off the production line is measured in years rather than months.

The idea behind simultaneous engineering is to attend to all the aspects at the same time. Once an idea for a new product has been accepted, the project is handed to a **special project team**, which assumes responsibility until first deliveries. The team contains people from all areas – design, marketing, production, engineering, manufacturing and purchasing. Instead of each department completing its task before passing it to another, the team acts simultaneously.

Whilst the design is being finalised, the marketing implications are relayed to produce further refinements. At the same time, production engineers start working on manufacture, teaming up with design engineers to facilitate production. The purchasing department and engineers work with suppliers to incorporate their ideas.

The team approach provides an excellent way of getting around the delays that hamper introducing a product. Decisions can be taken quickly, inter-departmental conflicts are readily resolved, and clear lines of authority are established.

This contrasts with the procedures of some Western companies that have tended to sling the product together and sort out the problems after launch! For example, in the motor industry consumers have been wise not to buy the first model of a new car. The Japanese way is to spend more time on conceiving the product so that it is virtually free of problems by the time it reaches the consumer. Honda, for example, has cut two years from the five-year development cycle needed to introduce a car.

The results from Western companies that have tried simultaneous engineering have been remarkable. American Telephone and Telegraph halved the time it took to produce a new cordless telephone. Hewlett-Packard cut the time it took to develop a new laser printer from four-and-a-half years to 22 months.

The product that is first in the market often becomes the one that will become the standard the others will be forced to emulate.

Task 1
What benefits might a company reap if they practise simultaneous engineering?

Task 2
What difficulties do you see in trying to introduce simultaneous engineering in Western companies?

Task 3

How does simultaneous engineering help companies to become more marketing orientated?

Combining marketing and financial objectives

In the previous case study we saw that successful planning involves all areas of company activity. We can now see how marketing and financial objectives can be brought together in a **total marketing plan**. The financial objective of a company may be tied up with strategic goals of the company related to profit making and growth. For example, a company may seek to maximise long term revenues for shareholders. In order to achieve this, the company may set the marketing objective of clearly identifying the target market for its product and doing its utmost to satisfy the market. For example, Pedigree Petfoods, the leading producers of petfood in this country, state that:

'We work constantly towards identifying and satisfying consumer needs. It is the activity from which all else springs. We never forget that we cannot influence millions of consumer

Figure 12.1
Developing a marketing plan

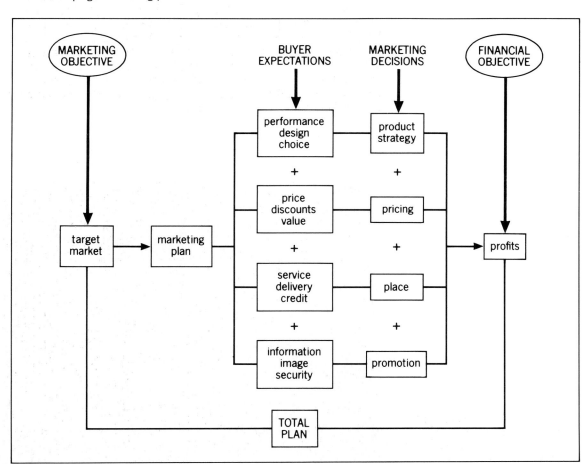

choices until we have convinced first one, then a second and a third consumer that our product is worthy of purchase. Our success is based on thorough research of the wide range of needs for pet animals and their owners. The knowledge which we gain is translated into a range of quality products which satisfy these needs better than any of our competitors.'

Developing an effective marketing plan (see figure 12.1) therefore involves investigating buyer expectations in order to make effective decisions about *Product*, *Price*, *Place*, and *Promotion*. If the plan is effective then not only will consumers be satisfied, but the strategic objectives of the company will be realised in terms of meeting financial and other objectives.

CASE STUDY

Marketing 'The Peterborough Effect'

During the 1980s one of the most successful areas in the United Kingdom was Peterborough. Peterborough developed a clear strategy for the growth and development of the town. The clarity of the strategy made it possible to pursue precise operational targets for growth and development. The engine behind much of the success was skilful marketing. 'The Peterborough Effect' was the marketing slogan employed to promote the expansion of the New Town of Peterborough. By studying this case you should look at the objectives that Peterborough established and how it was able to follow these through in long term and short term planning. The case study highlights many of the key themes of the book: identifying a target market, segmenting your market, and selecting the marketing mix that best suits your aims.

Figure 12.2
An example of an advert that was part of the ongoing campaign to market 'The Peterborough Effect'.

In 1967, Peterborough was designated a New Town; building began in 1970. During this time the 'Greater Peterborough Master Plan' was published laying the basis for the future growth of the city by Peterborough Development Corporation, in partnership with the City and County Councils.

Peterborough was to expand to meet three objectives:

1 To contribute directly to the relief of London's severe housing congestion by providing homes.

2 To absorb some of the huge natural increase in population occurring in the South East.

3 'To effect large and rapid improvements in the existing City structure and to provide facilities for the benefit of its present and future citizens' (quote from Development Plan).

Since 1970, then, Peterborough has had a policy of growth. Job creation was to be the engine house to power the dramatic growth – almost doubling the population from 81 000 to 150 000 in 20 years.

The task for the authorities has been to create a new, high quality regional city, with a vastly increased housing stock, creating thousands of new jobs, expanding and enhancing all local facilities and improving the quality of the overall city environment.

To effect these changes, the Development Corporation was given wide ranging powers – and importantly the finance to make development possible.

The Corporation was empowered to:

● purchase and develop land

● provide sites and premises for industrial and office developments

● provide new homes

● provide new leisure facilities.

However, the Development Corporation couldn't sit back and wait for the companies to arrive. Many new companies would need to be attracted to provide the jobs required and a marketing effort would be needed to tell the outside world the benefits of moving to Peterborough.

At the time Peterborough was not the logical choice for young, dynamic and expanding companies. Rather, it was thought to be a dull town with two railway stations and a large diesel engine manufacturer, Perkins. It was a city through which one passed on a railway journey or passed by on the A1.

Coupled with this was a downturn in the economy. As a result, an aggressive, skilful and expensive marketing strategy was required if companies were to be attracted and if the targets for employment growth were to be met.

The facts that lay behind the negative image had to be confronted. The marketing message would have to encompass all the attributes of the city.

Peterborough had, or would have:

- ready built factories and offices
- more and better jobs
- regional shopping
- leisure facilities
- a first-class range of new homes
- roads and cycleways
- a new landscape
- safe footpaths.

Peterborough needed a marketing statement to embrace all the new development activity and the new opportunities. That statement was:

> **THE PETERBOROUGH EFFECT**

Promoting the Peterborough Effect

This message had to be conveyed to the right people in the wide market of companies. In the case of the jobs market they needed to be clear about what firms they were trying to attract and how they were going to attract them.

To a certain extent the type of companies had already been determined. Peterborough had a range of offices and a wide selection of factory units to fill. The targets were therefore small and large office-based organisations and small-medium manufacturing and distribution firms, with facilities for both to expand substantially.

Having established a market, research needed to be carried out into what companies wanted. The main criteria (in no particular order) were:

- good communications by road, rail, air or sea
- a ready available skilled, adaptable workforce
- trouble free labour relations
- suitable land or modern property
- a choice of reasonably priced homes
- schools with a good academic record.

So, having identified targets it was necessary to persuade the target companies to come to the area. There were a number of marketing techniques that could be employed:

- Advertising – TV and Press
- Exhibitions
- Public Relations
- Direct Mail.

Advertising is very expensive. At the time, a well-produced 30 second TV commercial would have cost at least £80 000 and each showing on Channel 4 around £4000. Each showing on Thames TV at peak times cost £35 000.

Advertising can be exciting, dramatic, artistic and amusing. However, if it didn't provoke the person who saw it or read it to send for some information or to visit Peterborough then it would have failed.

The marketing department of the Development Corporation felt that the advertising needed to be:

Relevant – did it tell the viewer or reader what they wanted to know?

Simple – could the message be absorbed and understood in 30 seconds (in the case of a TV commercial).

Provocative – would it provoke the viewer/reader into making a response?

It was felt that the adverts would require repetitive showings over several months to be effective. In the end it was decided to produce several versions of television advertisements to be shown on Channel 4. The advertisements stressed features such as communications, housing and leisure.

Over the years the advertisements followed a number of themes, but all stressed 'The Peterborough Effect'. In the late 1980s the advertisements were designed to incorporate the Roman theme (see figure 12.2) to emphasise that Peterborough, while a new city, has a history.

The main thrust of the advertising concentrated on **the press**. By careful choice of newspaper and selection of the appropriate geographical region, a pre-determined target audience was reached. Again, it was not cheap.

A small inside page advertisement in the *Financial Times* cost £4500 (1988). A full page in the *Sunday Times* cost over £30 000.

It is difficult to assess success or failure in such campaigns. However, a response mechanism was built into the adverts. For the television adverts interested parties were invited to respond by use of the Freephone and coupons were attached to press adverts.

Peterborough's marketers also used some more direct methods. Advertising is very much an 'arms length' form of marketing – hold your breath and hope you get a response. **Exhibitions** are very much more direct providing that you can get people to go to them.

Each year, Peterborough Development Corporation held a major exhibition in London and invited an audience from target companies, city institutions, accountants, bankers, estate agents and property surveyors; in other words all those in a position to influence the decision to locate or relocate a company.

Public relations was another direct means of promoting the city. Throughout the objective of the marketing campaign was to get the city talked about in a positive manner. Good press relations were essential. Good editorial coverage can be more effective, create more impact, and yield more enquiries than advertising. So, the Development Corporation contained a small Public Relations and Press section constantly keeping the media in touch with new developments and news.

Finally, the development corporation produced a wide range of up-to-date literature which was sent out to a range of organisations.

The range of marketing tools that have been described above were used constantly whether individually or together. Each was felt to be vital to the effective promotion of Peterborough.

Peterborough has become one of the boom towns of the 1980s by attracting a wide range of large and small companies. This progress continues into the 1990s.

Task 1

What was the strategy used to market Peterborough?

Identify some of the key tactics employed in pursuit of this marketing strategy.

Task 2

Why was it important for the Peterborough Development Corporation to involve itself in marketing activities?

What was the target market selected by the marketing department?

Task 3

What did market research reveal about the requirements of the target market?

Task 4

What images were used to attract the target audience?

Task 5

What marketing techniques were felt to be most useful in promoting Peterborough?

Do you think that the Peterborough marketing plan was a success? Why?

Task 6

The marketing department of the Development Corporation used the slogan 'The Peterborough Effect' to encapsulate everything that was important about developing Peter-borough. What other slogans are you aware of that incorporate key features of company image? For example, something like 'You can be sure of Shell!' encapsulates an image of quality and reliability. Explore six other famous slogans.

Planning for tomorrow

Planning is taking decisions today about what is to be done tomorrow. Forward thinking is imperative if a company is going to be successful in meeting its goals. In 1990, Gillette already boasted a 62.5% value share of the UK wet-shave market and a 67% value share in North America and Europe. However, this does not mean that it rests on its laurels with existing products. Throughout the 1980s Gillette was researching and testing new products for the 1990s. Gillette (like Coca-Cola and Kodak) is a believer in global advertising. In February 1991 Gillette simultaneously launched its new razor, Sensor in 19 countries (see figure 12.3).

The same commercial will be used throughout North America and Europe. A new slogan was developed for the Contour campaign: "Gillette. The best a man can get".

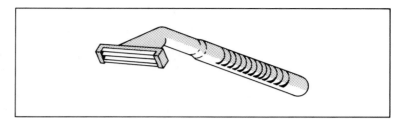

Figure 12.3
The Gillette campaign

The most important reason for planning is the possibility of change and uncertainty. If marketing took place in a safe and predictable environment then planning would not be difficult. However, change is ever-present and needs to be accounted for.

The uncertain butter market

Twenty years ago, butter seemed to have a safe future in a large market (ie for yellow fat producers). Today, butter has come to be seen in the same light as chocolate and cream – a luxury (see figure 12.4). It is high in calories, costs more than rival products and has a high cholesterol-content. In a climate of concern over health and diet, Flora and low-fat butter substitutes are more likely to figure in shopping lists than some well known butters.

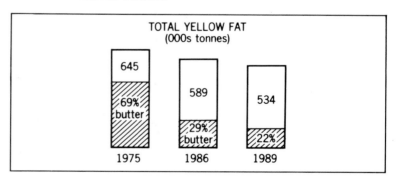

Figure 12.4
The market for total yellow fat

When Flora was launched in 1965 no-one would have foreseen the success it enjoys today. Now, butter must make plans against an uncertain future. These changes are reflected in the amount spent on advertising. £11m goes on advertising butter, more than double spent on margarines and low-fat spreads. The reality is that butter is still used in most households but on fewer and fewer occasions. Research shows that while 70% of UK households still use butter, it is just one of many yellow fats in the average fridge. Butter has had to seek a new strategy to counteract the onslaught of margarine.

The latest strategy for butter abandons the traditional imagery of cows, green fields and milkmaids which have been usurped to a large extent by the new rivals. Instead, it concentrates on discovering butter for the first time. One of the new commercials features a polar bear sniffing a rose which has grown up miraculously through the pack ice. The viewer is then asked to 'Imagine if you'd never smelt a rose. . . . Imagine if you'd never tasted butter.' Up comes a shot of butter melting on a corn cob.

Planning helps to bring your objectives out into the open. There is a famous saying that 'if you don't know where you are going then any road will take you there'. The point is that without clear planning you may achieve something, but it is unlikely to amount to much. If company objectives are clarified then individual departments have clear guidelines and it is possible for all departments to work in a co-ordinated way.

Planning also makes it possible for management to evaluate performance. Without evaluation you have no control. Of course, plans are unlikely to be met in every detail. However, they establish guidelines against which performance can be checked and if necessary modified.

Planning should be a continuous process. A useful model (although not the only one), is to establish objectives, clarify the planning assumptions that are being made, collect and sort out useful data, evaluate alternative courses of action, select an appropriate course of action, then re-evaluate the chosen course, and modify planning in the light of results (see figure 12.5).

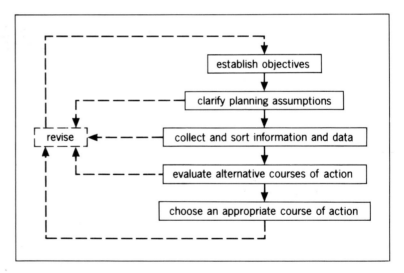

Figure 12.5
Preparing and revising plans

Another way of approaching planning involves the following:

Diagnosis Where are we and why? This usually involves some form of audit of company performance, which will then be analysed.

Prognosis Where are we going? This involves looking at possible future scenarios in the light of present performance and trends.

Objectives Where do we want to go? What is important?

Strategy What is the best way of achieving our objectives?

Tactics What specific actions will enable us to meet day-to-day targets.

Control How far have we progressed? A company will need to establish performance indicators against which it can measure its success.

Producing a marketing plan

The marketing plan in a large company will consist of a number of plans made by each of the sub-groups within a marketing department. It will be a compromise between the long term corporate plan of the company and shorter range plans. Elements of the marketing plan will be:

The product mix plan

This will set out which products should be phased out, which products should be modified, which new products will enter the portfolio and at what time. It should set out objectives for volume of sales, turnover and profits. It should establish how each of the products will be supported within the company, for example by sales staff.

Pricing plan

Pricing is important for any company. The pricing plan should set out the principles that cover pricing and discounting of products. Lower prices don't always mean more or better business. It may be better to build a sound long term business than price to attract short term or specific orders. If in doubt, it usually makes sense to price high as you can always reduce price or give special offers. If you price low you will find it difficult to put up the price in the short period. It could also put you out of business. The pricing plan should answer questions such as 'Do we need big volume turnover and can we manage it?' and 'Do we need to aim for lower volume with a bigger margin?'

Physical distribution plan

As we saw in the chapter on distribution, effective channels can give a critical competitive edge. Where physical distribution costs are relatively high it is important to use the most effective channels, to control stock efficiently and to minimise breakages and delays. The physical distribution plan needs to be integrated with other key areas of the marketing mix.

Promotional plan

In many large companies, promotions will be tied to the lifecycle of a product. Promotional activity will be required at launch, and periodically to inject new life into a product.

Promotion will also be closely tied to seasonal fluctuations and other short term influences on demand. Advertising will be a key ingredient of the promotional plan. Advertising is only a very small part of promotion. Advertising on its own seldom, if ever, succeeds.

A satisfied customer is the best form of advertising and planning thus has a lot in common with market research in that the aim is to be consumer-led.

The market research plan

Market research planning is particularly important for products whose nature and market are constantly changing. The market research plan will cover three main areas:

- Gathering of market data.
- Constantly checking on performance in the market place, as well as the performance of competitors.
- Regularly testing products, markets, operations and ideas.

The sales plan

Many organisations will also have a discrete sales plan. This will set out targets and planned activities for the sales function in areas such as customer service, and sales penetration. Specific plans are likely to be formulated for given groups of customers and specific accounts.

The advertising plan

Large organisations may also have advertising plans which are separate from other promotional plans. However, the two will clearly need to complement each other. The advertising plan will contain details of which media to concentrate on, how to allocate the advertising budget, the type of audience to be reached, procedures for tracking the success of campaigners and other features.

CASE STUDY

Planning a new product line

This case study provides you with information about the launch of Persil washing-up liquid in September 1990. The tasks that follow ask you to identify some of the planning procedures that would have been behind this development. You may find it helpful to attempt some extra research before completing them.

'Persil washes whiter' is a slogan that can have bypassed few of us since the 1950s. Now we have a new proposition: Persil also washes dishes.

Persil washing-up liquid was launched in September 1990 with an £8 million advertising campaign aimed squarely at the undisputed champion of the kitchen sink, Fairy Liquid.

In 1989, Fairy took on Persil on its home turf, by launching an automatic washing powder and liquid. This has led to a counter-offensive by Persil. The initiative is bound to stir up the long-running battle between the two largest companies that make up the detergent market, Lever Brothers and Procter & Gamble. Fairy (owned by Procter & Gamble) accounts for half the £120m Britain spends on washing-up liquid each year. Lever's Persil, on the other hand, accounts for sales of £192 million per year.

Inevitably this will have repercussions. Procter & Gamble is recognised by many to be one of the world's most dynamic marketing organisations. Marketing tactics at Procter & Gamble are concerned with giving products a high visibility, clear branding, and an aggressively competitive edge.

In 1989, Procter & Gamble discovered that Lever planned to launch a new detergent, Radion, with the promise that it would remove 'stale odours'. Before the Radion advertising had hit television screens, Procter & Gamble was on air with its own commercial for Ariel Automatic which asked a housewife if her clothes smelled. 'Don't be daft,' she replied. 'I use Ariel'.

The new Persil washing-up liquid is targeted at the 'premium, concentrated', segment of the market, a direct challenge to Fairy. Persil's product will reflect the 'caring and family values' that Persil claims to represent.

Task 1
Identify planning areas that would be involved in planning the new Persil washing-up liquid. Explain the sorts of plans you would expect to be made in these areas.

Task 2
What would you expect to be the key ingredients in the strategy of a detergent giant?

Task 3
What tactical decisions would support such a strategy?

Task 4
Why do you think that Lever have decided to extend the Persil brand?

Conclusion

In this chapter, we have set out to show that marketing planning is crucial to success and that it underpins the whole process of corporate planning. Marketing activities are carried out to meet organisational objectives shaped by the market place. The pursuit of marketing objectives should lead to an effective and efficient use of resources both for individual organisations and for society. They should also maximise returns in terms of the objectives set.

The company should know where it is going while always being prepared to adjust rapidly. The market-place moves on. For example, in the 1960s not many people would have imagined that in the 1990s middle-aged men in 'comfy' cardigans and cavalry twills would have become the battle-ground for the fashion industry. A recent marketing survey has revealed that the over-fifties have a disposable income of £108 million a year (1990), more than the entire contents of the nation's building societies and double that of the 16–34s. Not only are the over-fifties affluent, their numbers are increasing even as teenagers disappear. This particular age group is known in the clothing trade as the 'grey market'. Stylish clothes for the 'fuller figure' are becoming a key new growth area for clothing designers. The Burton Group has resurrected its 56 year old company, Huttons – selling suits and casual wear. Not to be outdone, the 102-year old Dunn and Company, which boasts a customer base of 19 to 90, has called in an image specialist to update its look without alarming some of its more 'sober' customers.

So, marketing planning needs to carefully look ahead, to foresee future trends and to plan for them!

CHAPTER

13

Marketing in Practice — A Case Study in Strategic Marketing

So how does strategic marketing work in practice? Let's have a detailed look at an actual case.

In the 1986 budget the Chancellor of the Exchequer announced a new, tax-free way for the public to invest in shares of publicly-owned companies. The name of this scheme was the 'Personal Equity Plan.'

Most of the leading investment management companies in Britain considered this a golden opportunity and launched such schemes. MIM Britannia, the company we will examine, was no exception.

Initially, MIM Britannia followed the rest of the industry and produced a brochure entitled 'The MIM Britannia Personal Equity Plan'.

The brochure began:

ALL YOU NEED TO KNOW: HOW TO TAKE ADVANTAGE OF A PERSONAL EQUITY PLAN WITH MIM BRITANNIA.

In the 1986 Budget, the Chancellor of the Exchequer announced a new scheme, Personal Equity Plans, to encourage the British public to take a greater interest in the country's leading companies, by actually investing in those companies' shares. To encourage this investment in British industry, the Chancellor announced important tax concessions.

If you analyse that statement, you will see that it consists of product features, not consumer benefits. However, this approach was the norm for the industry and, over the first two years of the scheme, total sales throughout the industry were some £200 million with MIM Britannia achieving around £12 million of this total.

In late 1988 however, the company appointed a marketing strategist to the board and a complete review of the PEP product was undertaken.

The Market

First, the market as a whole was examined and assessed for potential.

(a) UK Savings & Investments Age 20–69 Accounts Held (percentage)

Socio-economic groups	Population	B/Soc	U/Trust	Bank a/c	Life Ins	Stocks
A	18	22	36.7	19.7	17.8	31.7
B						
C1	22	26.2	25	25.2	24	27.9
C2	27	27.4	18.4	28.3	31.7	22.4
D	18	15.4	10.1	16.2	17.8	10.4
E	15	9	9.8	10.6	8.7	7.6
	100	100	100	100	100	100

The importance of cultivating the C1C2 sector is clearly demonstrated in the above table.

The importance of advertising volume *may* also be indicated by the disproportionate holding of unit trusts by ABs to whom almost all unit trust advertising has, historically, been addressed. Even so, C1C2's account for 20% more of the accounts held, with greater potential for expansion than the heavily fought over ABs.

(b) The Potential PEP Market

Product Group	S/E Group	Millions
Regular Savings	BC1C2D	29.40
U.T. Capital	ABC	14.35

To assess volume of business it was assumed that the industry would achieve 10% market penetration over five years. MIM Britannia set itself the objective of becoming the market leader with a 10% share of the market. Converting this objective to hard numbers resulted in the following table:

Year	Annual Accounts	Decay	Net Cum A/cs	Annual Sales Value	Cum Value	5% Initial Margin	Management Fees	Initial Margin Reinvestment	Box Profits	Total Gross Margin
1	100 100	14 154	86 946	122 154 000	122 629 050	6 083 700	1 285 600	70 964	717 540	8 157 804
2	100 100	26 325	161 719	146 839 440	268 680 614	7 127 436	2 790 162	268 111	964 394	11 150 103
3	100 100	36 705	226 023	168 068 880	441 922 656	8 392 524	4 625 947	517 084	1 176 688	14 712 243
4	100 100	45 797	281 325	186 326 160	641 209 358	9 678 060	6 679 712	819 220	1 359 261	18 536 253
5	100 100	53 539	328 885	202 027 440	868 051 385	10 981 212	9 003 630	1 177 528	1 516 274	22 678 644

You will note that the company was essentially aiming to equal the sales of the whole industry from day one! It will be further apparent that this industry operates on very narrow profit margins, there is no room for error.

The next step was to assess the distribution costs of the product. There were three methods of distribution available, advertising methods, via intermediaries (insurance brokers, stock brokers, solicitors, accountants), and direct mail.

The three routes were assessed as follows:

(a) Promotional Costs

(i) Advertising

Assumptions

The required advertising spend was based upon the 1988 unit trust and life assurance press advertising spend. TV is, at this stage, ignored. It was assumed that media costs would grow by 10% per annum and industry advertising volume by 5% per annum.

It was further assumed that 30% of industry advertising spend would be committed to PEP based products.

To achieve a given level of market penetration it is often accepted that if you outspend your competitors, you will always win in the long term. Thus, with a target of 10% share a 12% share of spend was projected.

Projected Adspend (1988 = £64 million) £ millions

Year	1	2	3	4	5
1 Industry Total	73.6	84.6	97.3	111.9	128.7
2 PEP @ 30% of 1	22.1	25.3	29.2	33.6	38.6
3 MIM @ 12% of 2	2.64	3.05	3.50	4.03	4.63

Production

The company's advertising experience would indicate that the cost per contract is as follows:

	Cost per Enquiry	% Conversion	Cost per Conversion
Savings	£15	15	£100
UT Capital	£25	15	£166
PEP	£50	10	£500

Thus, if these production rates were not improved and the advertising campaign were evenly spread over the three areas (unlikely) the annual production would be as follows:

Product	No of Contracts
Savings	8 800
UT Capital	5 300
PEP	1 760

(ii) Intermediary Sales

Assumptions

It was assumed that 25% of all PEP business is introduced via agents and that an initial commission of 3% is paid with renewals of 0.5% from year 2 onwards.

The commission commitment on the business figures projected in the table above would therefore be as follows.

Total Year	Initial	Renewal	Total
1	912 555		912 555
2	1 069 115	191 953	1 261 068
3	1 258 878	408 506	1 667 384
4	1 451 709	657 614	2 109 323
5	1 647 181	941 187	2 588 368

(iii) Direct Mail

To achieve the corporate target, direct mail had to be the business source to fill the shortfall between the sum of advertising production and intermediary production and the target numbers.

On the bases used, this annual shortfall is:

Product	No of Contracts
Savings	36 050
UT Capital	16 225
PEP	7 690

Assumptions

It was assumed that the cost per package was initially 35p and that a conversion rate of 0.5% would be experienced.

To achieve the business levels required, the direct mail quantities/costs in year 1 would be as follows.

Product	Quantity	Cost £
Savings	7 210 000	2 523 500
UT Capital	3 245 000	1 135 750
PEP	1 538 000	538 300
Total	11 993 000	4 197 550

Allowing an annual increase in costs of 10% the direct mail commitment would therefore be:

Year	Direct Mail Cost
1	4 197 550
2	4 617 305
3	5 079 035
4	5 586 939
5	6 145 632

(iv) Thus the total sales cost at the business levels projected was:

Year	Advertising	Direct Mail	Commission	Total
1	2 640 000	4 197 550	912 555	7 750 105
2	3 050 000	4 617 305	1 261 068	8 928 313
3	3 500 000	5 079 035	1 667 384	10 246 419
4	4 030 000	5 586 939	2 109 323	11 726 262
5	4 630 000	6 145 632	2 588 368	13 364 000

(b) Administrative Costs

(i) Material Costs

The fixed costs of processing PEP applications were estimated to be as follows:

Savings Plan × 1000

Acknowledgement	20.00
Acknowledgement Postage	145.00
R.P.E.	145.00
Direct Debit Postage	145.00
	455.00

Capital Products × 1000

Acknowledgement	20.00
Acknowledgement Postage	145.00
Formal Acknowledgement	20.00
Certificate	50.00
F.A. Postage	145.00
	380.00

The annual costs of maintaining PEP contracts were estimated to be:

Unit Trust Products × 1000

Item	Cost
Half yearly statement × 2	10.00
Managers Report × 2	360.00
Postage × 2	280.00
	740.00

Equity PEPs

Item	Cost
Quarterly Statement × 4	240
Postage ×	560
	800

(ii) Staffing Costs

The variable costs incurred in managing PEPs essentially relate to staffing.

It was estimated that 1 extra staff member would be required for every 2 500 equity PEPs or 5 000 unit trust PEPs up to 100 000 contracts above which 1 extra staff member would be required for each 5 000 equity PEPs or 10 000 unit trust PEPs.

Assumptions

An existing base of 36 000 contracts was allowed. It was assumed that each staff member earned £12 500 per annum and a further 50% (£6 250) added to cover benefits. Accommodation and expenses was estimated at £10 000 per annum. It was further assumed that there were currently 10 staff employed to administer PEPs.

Staff requirements and costs at the end of the year would thus be:

Year	Net Cumulative acs	Staff nos	£ Staff cost	£ Average annual admin cost per contract
1	86 946	19	521 250	5.99
2	161 719	27	711 250	4.40
3	226 023	33	853 750	3.78
4	281 325	39	996 250	3.54
5	328 885	43	1 091 250	3.32

(iii) Thus the total administrative cost at the business levels projected would be:

Year	Initial Costs £	Annual Costs £	Staff Costs £	Total £
1	42 903	63 716	521 250	627 869
2	42 903	120 882	711 250	875 035
3	42 903	168 407	853 750	1 065 060
4	42 903	210 284	996 250	1 249 437
5	42 903	245 833	1 091 250	1 379 986

(iv) Capital Costs

The hardware used to administer PEPs required upgrading at a cost of some £350 000.

(c) Profit Potential

At the business levels, margins and cost projected, the following net contributions would be achieved.

Year	Cumulative Value £	Total Gross Revenue	Sales Costs	Admin Costs	Net Contribution	% of Cumulative Funds
1	122 629 050	8 157 804	7 750 105	627 869	−220 170	−0.18
2	268 680 614	11 150 103	8 928 313	875 035	1 346 755	0.50
3	441 922 656	14 712 243	10 246 419	1 065 060	3 400 764	0.76
4	64 1209 358	18 536 253	11 726 262	1 249 437	5 560 554	0.88
5	868 051 385	22 678 644	13 364 000	1 379 986	7 934 658	0.91

However, these numbers were based upon an historic promotional spend of around £400 000 so the expectations were revised to allow for the large projected increase.

In practice, increased professionalism and more careful testing and targeting of the advertising should improve the conversion rates. Realistic targets were considered to be:

Savings	30%
UT Capital	20%
PEP	10%